Beyond Survival Mode

Beyond Survival Mode

THRIVING AS A TRAUMA-INFORMED PROFESSIONAL

Megan Corcoran

amba press

Published in 2026 by Amba Press, Melbourne, Australia
www.ambapress.com.au

Cover design: Tess McCabe
Internal design: Amba Press
Editor: Brooke Lyons

ISBN: 9781923403727 (pbk)
ISBN: 9781923403734 (ebk)

A catalogue record for this book is available from the National Library of Australia.

Praise

This is an outstanding and clear-cut guide for professionals to create systems and deliver practice that meets children where they truly are, based on up-to-date, robust science. An urgent gamechanger for children and those who serve them.

Benjamin Perks, author of Trauma Proof: Healing, Attachment and the Science of Prevention

There is a lifetime's experience in this book, and it shows in lessons learnt and wisdom shared. *Beyond Survival Mode* is an easy read, packed with workable strategies. I can't wait to add it to my 'best-loved' collection of resources.

Marg Thorsborne, author, practitioner, trainer

This book is for every educator who breathes air. Essential reading for those doing the most important work in the world.

Thea Stinear, CEO, CoolPlus

Beyond Survival Mode is a compassionate and thought-provoking account of what it means to teach, lead and learn through trauma-informed principles. I recommend this book to all educators seeking an authentic and accessible companion on the journey towards trauma-informed growth and change.

Jack Greig, Senior Advisor – Leadership and Research, Berry Street Education Model

Megan has placed herself as an observer, like the infamous fly on the wall, watching the impact of trauma both for the person hurt and those within their social and support circles. A great read, and certainly adds to my knowledge and understanding.

Richard Rose, Director, Therapeutic Life Story Work International (TLSWi)

Reading this book felt like hiking a mountain – each chapter builds thoughtfully on the last, and when you reach the top, the view is clear. *Beyond Survival Mode* brings together personal story, science and actionable practice to illuminate our shared responsibility for wellbeing.

Annemarie Holmyard, experienced educator

Megan draws on her extensive experience and deep understanding of implementing wellbeing practices in schools and organisations across Australia and far beyond. She advocates for a collective approach to staff wellbeing and offers practical strategies to embed within the everyday rhythms of campus life.

Associate Professor Tom Brunzell, University of Melbourne

Contents

About the Author

Megan Corcoran is a trauma-informed wellbeing consultant, educator and writer, and the Founder and Director of Wagtail Institute. She works alongside schools, community organisations and complex settings to strengthen staff wellbeing, culture and practice in environments shaped by trauma and chronic stress.

With a background in alternative and flexible education, Megan has spent much of her career supporting children and young people who have experienced significant childhood trauma, alongside the adults who care for and teach them. Her work is grounded in the belief that we cannot sustainably support young people unless we also attend to the wellbeing, competency and working conditions of the adults around them.

Megan holds a master's degree in Applied Positive Psychology (MAPP) with a focus on trauma, wellbeing and belonging. She integrates trauma-informed practice, wellbeing science and relational approaches into practical, human-centred frameworks that translate evidence into everyday action.

She is also the host of the *Wag Tales* podcast, where she shares conversations about trauma, healing, education and wellbeing with practitioners, researchers and lived-experience voices from around the world.

Above all, Megan is committed to helping organisations move beyond survival mode, creating systems and cultures where people can feel safe, valued and supported to do meaningful work, together.

Introduction

I deeply believe that all children and young people deserve a safe and magical childhood, supported by adults who believe in their future. For me, those adults were my grandparents, Max and Phyllis.

Not all children and young people find those adults in their homes or their families. Sometimes, they find those adults in schools, youth centres or sporting clubs. No matter where those adults show up, all children deserve to find them.

This belief is what led me to become a teacher, and to take a graduate role in an alternative high school, working alongside young people living in out-of-home care. It continued to guide me as I moved into school leadership roles, and when I founded the Wagtail Institute.

I have spent close to 20 years working in education and complex systems, and I truly believe teaching is one of the best jobs in the world. I have seen schools change lives. I have seen educators stand beside children and young people through grief, chaos and harm, and support them to find steadier ground.

It is incredibly rewarding work, but it asks a great deal of us.

Over time, I began to notice a pattern: the adults doing this work were showing extraordinary care, commitment and resilience, often at a significant personal cost. I saw talented, values-driven professionals becoming exhausted, overwhelmed and disillusioned, or leaving roles they once loved.

I wore plenty of that personal cost myself, particularly as a school leader. I was absorbed by the work, treating it with urgency and 100 per cent commitment. I normalised an 'activated stress state', and found I performed well under pressure. It was almost addictive, but incredibly unsustainable.

We cannot build safe, healing environments for young people if the adults within those environments are operating in survival mode.

This book was written for the adults who show up every day in trauma-affected spaces. Teachers. Leaders. Practitioners. Support workers. Carers. It is for those who care deeply, who believe in the young people they support, and who want to keep doing this important work, sustainably.

I needed a way to make sense of what actually helps people stay well in the midst of complex, trauma-impacted work. After supporting thousands of professionals across Australia and the UK, this work developed into the Wagtail Wellbeing NEST framework.

NEST invites us to:

- **Notice** what is happening within ourselves, our teams and our systems
- **Embed** practices that support safety, regulation and clarity into everyday work
- **Strengthen** relationships, belonging and shared responsibility
- **Thrive** by creating the conditions for growth, purpose and joy.

Beyond Survival Mode is an invitation to think differently about our wellbeing, our trauma-informed practice and what it actually takes to sustain this work over time. We will explore how trauma and chronic stress affect our bodies, our relationships and our workplaces, and how we can respond in ways that are preventative, relational and human.

Note that this book represents a moment in time, a point in my own learning journey, and offers just one small piece in the broader trauma-informed puzzle. While writing this book, the science of this work continued to develop and I'll be forever learning and unlearning, too.

As you read on, you will find theory alongside stories. Research alongside reflection. Practical strategies alongside questions worth sitting with. Some chapters will invite you to look inwards; others outwards, towards the systems and cultures we are part of. You do not need to read this book from start to finish, or agree with everything in it. I hope that you take what is useful, leave what is not and return to it as needed.

This book invites us all to move beyond survival mode, where we can create something far more powerful – for ourselves, and for the children and young people who are counting on us.

Part I

Notice

notice *verb*
to become aware of, esp. by looking; to see.

Cambridge Dictionary

We begin by noticing the impact of trauma and adversity in the lives of the people we support, and in our own lives. We pay attention to how trauma shows up in behaviours, relationships, team dynamics and systems.

We also learn to notice what is already present and working. The strengths people draw on to survive. The moments of connection, care, humour and persistence. The skills, values and capacities that often go unseen in environments shaped by stress.

This stage is about naming what's real, reducing shame and creating a shared understanding that becomes the foundation for change.

When we widen what we notice, we move away from deficit-based stories and towards a more complete human picture – one that allows us to respond with greater compassion, clarity and hope.

1

Wet Socks and the Case for Trauma-Informed Wellbeing

Every child deserves to have a safe and magical childhood, supported by adults who believe in their future. If you're reading this book, you likely believe that quite deeply, too.

That belief is the reason I became a teacher. It's the reason I took a graduate position in an alternative school. And it remained my reason each time I made a new career decision.

But for the longest time, I overlooked what it actually takes to make that belief a reality.

Well adults.

Adults equipped with trauma-informed knowledge. Adults supported with skills and resources to stay well while doing this important work.

According to the Substance Abuse and Mental Health Services Administration (SAMHSA, 2014), being trauma-informed invites us to:

- **realise** how trauma shapes individuals, groups and communities
- **recognise** the signs, symptoms and wide-reaching impacts
- **respond** in ways that meet people's needs and promote healing
- **prevent** further harm or re-traumatisation.

And importantly, this work includes us, too.

This is why this book exists: to explore what it means to bring a trauma-informed lens to our own wellbeing, to our teams and to the communities we serve. When we understand these principles for ourselves, we are better placed to create environments where children and young people can genuinely thrive.

We will unpack trauma-informed practice more deeply in part II: Embed. For now, let's notice what is happening within our trauma-impacted workplaces and within ourselves.

Becoming trauma-informed: it's a journey, not a destination

> The expectation that we can be immersed in suffering and loss daily and not be touched by it is as unrealistic as expecting to be able to walk through water without getting wet.
>
> *Rachel Remen (1996).*

For too long, I think we liked to pretend we could support our trauma-impacted children and young people without feeling any of the impacts ourselves.

We thought we could stay dry while walking through water. Or at least, we chose to put up with the wet socks.

We have become skilled at applying trauma-informed practices *to* children and young people: helping them regulate, offering unconditional positive regard, supporting choice and voice.

But what we have not done well is incorporating trauma-informed wellbeing approaches with the adults doing the work: teachers, youth workers, social workers, residential carers, support workers, foster carers, allied health teams and sporting coaches.

What does it mean when we talk about *trauma-informed* wellbeing?

It's not just a bunch of catchy words.

You've probably heard the term 'trauma-informed' being used in your sector, and you may even be a part of a trauma-informed school or organisation.

But how trauma-informed are we?

In recent years, trauma-informed practice has gained momentum across various sectors, including education, healthcare, social services, corporate environments, online spaces and even in design. It's become a hallmark of progressive, compassionate practice, a term eagerly adopted by organisations and consultants alike.

But like many movements that gain popularity, its meaning risks becoming diluted, reduced to a buzzword stamped onto taglines and branding.

This movement, now almost a trend, aims to create safer, more supportive environments for everyone, acknowledging the pervasive impact of trauma on individuals and communities.

However, despite its widespread adoption, the depth and breadth of what it means to be truly trauma-informed is often misunderstood. It's not as simple as having an 'awareness' of the presence of trauma, nor is it just about attending a one-day professional development course to obtain a certificate.

The allure of being labelled as trauma-informed is undeniable. It signifies a school or organisation's commitment to understanding and mitigating the effects of trauma, promoting safety and wellbeing among staff and clients alike.

Yet the true essence of a trauma-informed approach goes beyond the surface level of catchy slogans and well-intentioned policies. It requires a profound shift in perspective, culture and practice. It's an ongoing journey rather than a destination.

The early days: applying trauma-informed practice to my students

My first teaching experience was in an alternative high school that provided education to young people living in out-of-home care. The school was only a few years old when I started, and the understanding of trauma-informed practice in schools was just emerging.

Back then, there was a misconception that these young people didn't want to attend school, so the school didn't even have the word 'school' in its name. It had been opened in a building that couldn't look less like a school: a converted warehouse with concrete floors and no natural light. Some of the staff members said we do 'education by stealth': get the young people in the door, treat them like they're in a youth centre and trick them into learning a few things.

Luckily for me (and our students), new ideas in the field were emerging quickly, and an exceptional principal was guiding our campus towards being a place where our students felt safe and could engage in meaningful education, without the trickery.

In the first few weeks, I was provided with some trauma training. It was helpful; it gave me insight into what trauma can do to the brain, why my students might behave in certain ways (the ways that we often label as 'challenging'), and strategies I could use to support these young people.

Trauma was presented to me as a big, dark cloud that loomed over my students. It was something rare, something that happened to them but not to many others. Something separate to me. They needed specialised practices to help them cope, and that's what trauma-informed education was all about.

In those early years, I *applied* trauma-informed practice to these young people. I used co-regulation strategies, met them with unconditional positive regard, provided them with choice and shared decision-making, saw their behaviour as reactions to their trauma and worked to understand their triggers.

And each day, I went home and took off my trauma-informed hat, imagining my own life existed outside the realm of trauma.

I believed trauma-informed practice was something *they* needed, not me. And that was a common belief in the field.

But, during those early days and weeks, I was also trying to teach myself how to walk through the water without getting wet. I was told that I might find the work emotionally challenging or stressful, but that I would learn to manage it, and it would stop impacting me over time. I was led to believe that those who stay in the field long-term are the ones who stop feeling the impacts.

So, I never mentioned my wet socks.

Ignoring the collective experience

The application-only approach misses something vital. Trauma is not just an individual experience; it is relational, collective and systemic. It affects all of us.

Using trauma-informed practices can be great in supporting others to feel safe, to create moments of co-regulation and to minimise harm, but it's not enough. We cannot use trauma-informed practice effectively if we see ourselves as separate from it.

Treating trauma as an individual issue disregards the systemic and relational aspects of trauma. We are all interconnected, and our experiences of trauma and healing influence one another.

We need to recognise:

- we are part of the relational system
- we shape and influence the environments around us
- we heal together; we are participants in the healing of ourselves and others
- we are impacted by the work.

Trauma is not just a clinical issue; it's a human experience. And when we acknowledge that, we begin to see trauma-informed practice for what it really is: *compassion in action*.

It's about understanding that we are all part of the same fabric, and healing is a journey we undertake together, shaping better environments, systems and policies along the way.

And, if we want to provide safe, supportive environments for the children and young people we are supporting, we *must* understand and invest in our own wellbeing, too.

Let's get clear on wellbeing

Too often in the helping professions, we speak of wellbeing as something we hold for others. We focus on improving student or client wellbeing. We show up consistently for the children and young people in our care. We think of wellbeing as something to build around them.

But too rarely do we ask what that means for *us*. Rarely do we ask how we build safety, connection and nourishment around ourselves.

For years, I didn't ask either. I assumed my wellbeing would take care of itself if I just worked hard enough. If I could stay calm, hold space and make it to the school holidays, I told myself I was doing fine.

The reality? I had no meaningful understanding of wellbeing beyond *not burning out.* And I wasn't alone.

How psychology shaped our narrow view of wellbeing

The idea that wellbeing is simply the absence of distress is deeply woven into the history of psychology itself.

The field of modern psychology was born in a time of crisis. It gained momentum during the 20th century against the backdrop of world wars, displacement and collective trauma. Its focus was on understanding what had gone wrong and how to repair it.

So, we learned to speak fluently about pain. We created names for disorders and detailed plans to manage them. We learned how to move away from suffering.

But not how to move towards wellbeing.

For a long time, the working assumption was: *if you're not unwell, you must be well.* Wellbeing became a linear line, zero on a scale, and all our systems were built to help people claw their way back to it.

Our understanding of psychology looked a little something like figure 1.

Figure 1: Traditional approach to psychology

-10	-5	0
Struggling with mental illness	Some experience of mental illness	No mental illness = well

Zero was the goal.

Zero meant you were functioning.

Zero meant you were *well.*

But zero is not enough. Wellbeing is not just the absence of illness. It's not just surviving, or getting through, or making it to the weekend. It's something richer and more expansive.

Before you read on, I'd like you to pause and think about the word 'wellbeing':

- How do you define it?
- How do you talk about it with your students, clients or colleagues?
- What does it mean in your daily life?

There is no single universal definition, but wellbeing science offers a widely accepted idea: 'Wellbeing is feeling good and functioning well' (Keyes & Annas, 2009).

Feeling good isn't just about happiness; it's about having a healthy emotional baseline and the capacity for positive experiences, relationships and connection.

Functioning well means showing up in our lives with competence, engagement, meaning and purpose.

And of course, these two feed each other. When we feel good, we function better. When we function well, we tend to feel better.

With the growing body of research in wellbeing science, we now get to look beyond that zero baseline (see figure 2, overleaf).

Figure 2: Presence of wellbeing

-10	0	+10
Struggling with mental illness	No mental illness	Presence of wellbeing

The trauma-informed wellbeing journey

Trauma impacts our capacity to feel good and function well. It disrupts our connection to ourselves, to others and to the world, which we will explore further in chapter 2.

On our trauma-informed journey, it's essential that we bring wellbeing science with us. If we set out with only the tools to prevent and respond to trauma, we'll make it partway, but eventually the supplies run out. We become stretched, tired and pushed back by the weight of the work.

But when we carry the tools that also strengthen us, nourish us and help us thrive, the journey changes. We're able to go further, with steadier steps and a fuller sense of who we are.

We must also understand that building safety, connection and supporting regulation in others is intimately tied to how we experience those things ourselves.

Wellbeing has to be something we practise, something we embody and something we invest in.

Completing the mental health picture

After a number of years working alongside my students, I began my Master of Applied Positive Psychology (MAPP), exploring the science of wellbeing.

Wellbeing science felt like a revelation – a reminder that we aren't here just to prevent harm, but to cultivate growth, hope and flourishing. I began applying some of the practices in my own life – gratitude journalling, learning about my character strengths and diving into self-compassion practices. Slowly, things shifted.

But a question kept following me through my studies:

- Where were my students, who had been impacted by trauma, in the research and frameworks?
- Where were the people like me who were exposed to stress and trauma in our workplaces?

If we look back at figure 2, it presents a binary picture: either you have an experience of illness *or* you have an experience of wellbeing.

The binary model, with illness on one end and wellbeing on the other, didn't reflect what I saw in real life. It didn't seem fair (or true) that wellbeing only begins once we're free of trauma or mental illness. I wanted more for the young people I was supporting, and honestly, my own experiences didn't fit on that singular line, either.

Amid my frustration in my studies, I did eventually experience a huge sigh of relief as I came across the work of Dr Corey Keyes and the dual continua model of mental health.

Figure 3: Adapted dual mental health continua

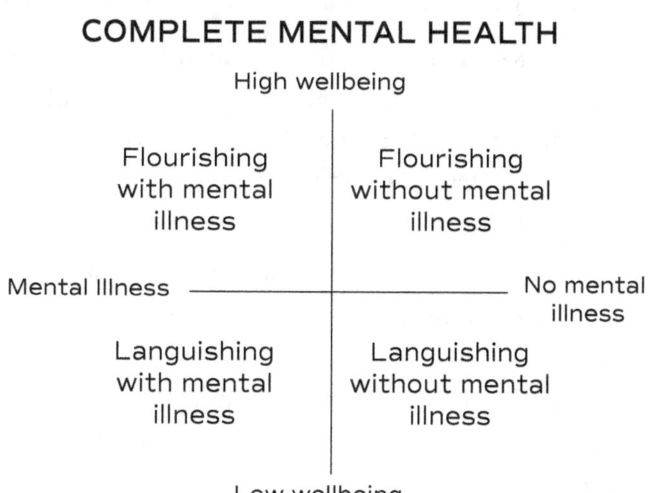

Adapted from Keyes (2002).

Keyes' model illustrates that mental illness and mental health are related but distinct. The model uses the terms 'flourishing' and 'languishing'.

Languishing is a feeling of aimlessness, emptiness and lack of vitality, characterised by the absence of mental wellbeing. This term gained a lot of traction during our lengthy COVID lockdowns, particularly here in Melbourne. At that time, I personally experienced languishing as I lost access to many of my usual wellbeing strategies, such as my boxing training and community, my regular dinner catch-ups with friends, and road trips out of the city.

In contrast, flourishing is a state of true wellbeing where individuals feel a sense of purpose, connection, personal growth and overall fulfilment.

For many, trauma sits on the illness axis. But trauma does not remove someone's capacity to flourish on the wellbeing axis.

A person can:

- experience mental illness and flourish
- have no mental illness and languish
- be healing and thriving at the same time.

A person can be thriving amid their healing, and healing amid their thriving – something many trauma-impacted people know intuitively.

I spoke with Corey Keyes in early 2025, and he shared something that has stayed with me. He explained that as he became more mentally healthy, his mental illness didn't disappear; it simply moved into the background, into the closet. Flourishing stepped into the foreground. Life felt fuller, richer, more connected. The illness was still there, just quieter.

There are days when our mental illness comes back out of the closet – not as a sign that we've failed or that we're back at the beginning, but simply because that's how being human works. On those days, Corey says we have to welcome it in. We don't slam the door on it. We don't pretend we're fine. We let it sit with us for a while and, in doing so, we create room for something new.

He described this through the lens of recovery. Recovery isn't the absence of symptoms; it's the process of building the things that contribute to our mental health and wellbeing. It's what we grow, not what we get rid of. And when our mental illness comes forward again, he says it's there to 'clean the house', to help us notice what needs attention, what needs clearing and what needs care.

The dual continua model serves as a powerful reminder: we can all learn the skills of wellbeing. We all deserve the resources and support to sustain it. And we all benefit from trauma-informed understanding and approaches to our wellbeing.

What's getting in the way of practitioner wellbeing?

Over the past few years, I've had the privilege of working with schools, youth centres, councils, mental health services and universities across Australia and the UK. At the time of writing, I've supported thousands of professionals and carers, and I have learned from every one of these interactions.

While every setting is unique, I've noticed consistent themes that compromise staff wellbeing, regardless of the sector. These themes include:

- trauma exposure without evidence-informed support
- behaviour of students or clients
- unsafe team culture
- unmanageable workload.

If you take a moment to consider what is compromising your wellbeing, it is likely the challenges can be mapped to one of these categories.

Furthermore, none of these challenges can be solved by individual wellbeing practices.

As practitioners, we often hold complex trauma, emotional labour and systems under strain. We are doing our best within environments that unintentionally reinforce burnout.

I've seen staff pushed to breaking point while being told to practise self-care as though meditation apps or gratitude journals can undo the damage of chronic stress, unsafe team dynamics or role ambiguity.

Wellbeing, like trauma, is not just personal – it's relational and systemic. When we are unsupported in the face of trauma exposure, when behaviour is managed rather than understood, when boundaries are blurred and team culture is unsafe, we can't expect people to just 'look after themselves'.

The work of trauma-informed wellbeing begins by recognising these deeper patterns and asking better questions. Instead of asking why staff aren't coping, we need to ask: *What are we doing, or not doing, that makes it so hard to thrive here?*

In the chapters ahead, we'll explore the root causes of practitioner distress and offer evidence-informed, relational, and practical ways we can do better, together.

Wagtail Wellbeing – building our NEST

Working in complex settings asks a lot of the humans who show up each day. It asks us to hold space for others while also navigating our own stories. It asks us to support healing while often working inside systems that can cause harm. And it asks us to care deeply, sometimes without having the structures in place that care for us.

This is where the Wagtail Wellbeing NEST framework comes in. It's a model developed through years of walking alongside educators, youth workers, mental health professionals and lived-experience teams. It's not a checklist or a program; it's a way of seeing and doing that helps us hold complexity with compassion. It's a roadmap I wish I had when I began supporting children and young people.

The framework weaves together trauma theory, wellbeing science and real-world practice. It recognises that for us to support healing in others, we need environments that are safe, connected and sustainable for ourselves. It invites us to move beyond surface-level wellbeing strategies and embed trauma-informed principles in meaningful, systemic ways.

Notice

We begin by noticing the impact of trauma and adversity in the lives of the people we support, and in our own lives. We pay attention to how trauma shows up in behaviours, relationships, team dynamics, and systems. We also learn to notice what is already present and working: the skills, values and capacities that often go unseen in environments shaped by stress. This stage is about naming what's real, reducing shame and creating a shared understanding that becomes the foundation for change.

Embed

We embed trauma-informed practice at every level of our work. This includes staff culture, leadership practices, workplace structures and the ways we respond to one another. We intentionally build safety, trust and empowerment, not only for the people accessing our services, but for those delivering them as well.

Strengthen

We strengthen our practices, relationships and systems so they can hold steady under pressure. This stage is about building capacity, resilience and alignment, ensuring that the principles of trauma-informed practice are lived out consistently, even when challenges arise. It's where leaders reinforce the conditions that allow their teams and communities to flourish.

Thrive

Trauma-informed practice is not only about reducing harm, it's about creating the conditions for growth, purpose and joy. In this final stage, we move beyond survival, drawing from the science of wellbeing and positive psychology. We focus on strengths, belonging, connection and meaning. We imagine what it looks like when individuals, teams and systems don't just cope, but truly thrive.

Throughout the book, we'll return to this roadmap. Each chapter will explore one part of the model in more depth, offering stories, strategies and reflections to help you bring trauma-informed wellbeing to life in your setting.

Chapter summary

- Trauma-informed practice is not about applying to others, but about being with others and being with ourselves.
- Wellbeing is not the absence of illness, but rather the presence of feeling good and functioning well.
- A person can flourish even while healing from trauma. Flourishing and illness can co-exist.
- Instead of asking why staff aren't coping, we need to ask: *what are we doing, or not doing, that makes it so hard to thrive here?*
- Individual wellbeing strategies cannot fix systemic issues. Wellbeing is relational and collective.
- For us to support healing in others, we need environments that are safe, connected, and sustainable.
- The Wagtail Wellbeing NEST acronym stands for: Notice, Embed, Strengthen and Thrive.

From insight to impact

- **Reflect on your current context.** What factors are shaping your wellbeing, both positively and negatively? Consider your team culture, leadership, workload and how supported you feel in your role. What's helping? What's hindering?
- **Reframe self-care.** Shift the focus from individual responsibility to shared accountability. Ask: *What would it look like if our team or organisation genuinely supported practitioner wellbeing?* What needs to be in place for that to happen?
- **Start conversations.** Use this chapter as a conversation-starter with colleagues or leaders. What parts resonate most with your experience? What feels realistic to shift? Where can you begin?

2

When Stress Sticks: Understanding Trauma, Adversity and Survival

This book is not going to take you through graphic or distressing stories. I do not believe we need to shock people into becoming trauma-informed. That approach might grab attention for a moment, but it can leave us feeling helpless, overwhelmed or even traumatised ourselves. And that goes against the very heart of this work.

Yes, we will define trauma. We will explore how it affects our body, our brain and our behaviour. We will notice how it can show up in the people we support, in ourselves, and across our workplaces and communities. I recognise even learning about the topic can be uncomfortable for some.

So before we go any further, I want to invite you into a stance of understanding and compassion – not only for others, but for yourself as well.

Living life in survival mode

> We know that we can't always ask our students to take off the armor at home, or even on their way to school, because their emotional and physical safety may require self-protection.

> But what we can do, and what we are ethically called to do as teachers, is create a space in our schools and classrooms where all students can walk in and, for that day or hour, take off the crushing weight of their armor, hang it on a rack, and open their heart to truly being seen.
>
> *Brown, 2018.*

I need to admit I am not a gamer, and I deeply apologise to any gamers if I get some of the details wrong in the following analogy.

I recently learned that the game Minecraft has the option to be played in survival mode or explore (create) mode.

In survival mode, players must manage resources, defend themselves, engage in combat, fight off hunger and dehydration, and find ways to build shelters and craft useful tools.

In explore mode, the focus is on discovery and freedom. Players engage in puzzles, use their creativity and build extra structures – not just shelters, but those that help advance the city.

Now, I couldn't think of a better analogy than what Minecraft gives us here.

Many of us have times when we are living life in survival mode. Our attention and focus is solely on what we need to survive in the day-to-day. We might be working multiple jobs to keep the roof over our heads, living under the threat of harm, navigating dangerous situations or experiencing toxic levels of stress.

We might need to manage our hunger, defend ourselves and craft tools (internal and external) to aid in our survival. When we are living life in survival mode, we might feel like it's moment-to-moment, day-to-day, just getting by.

In contrast, when we have the opportunity to live in explore mode, we find ourselves with more freedom and choice. We can engage in creative pursuits and use our imagination. We can rest, recharge and play. We can look beyond the moment-to-moment and the day-to-day, making plans for the future.

I've had times when I've experienced survival mode and, of course, times when I've experienced explore mode.

I've worked alongside too many young people who only know survival mode. And I've worked in organisations and schools that have been operating in survival mode.

Collective survival mode

When our workplaces get overwhelmed, we might find ourselves working in reactive ways. Our energy is placed in putting out spotfires, and the decisions we make are to manage the day, not to proactively build something better.

We forget our strategic plans, we lose the creativity and we lose the play. We're all working to get by; to manage the crisis of today.

When our society is overwhelmed, we find the collective functioning in reactive ways, too. The cost of living, housing insecurity, pandemics and global conflicts all impact the way we individually and collectively show up. Our internal systems and external systems start pumping an all-too-familiar stress.

We can see survival mode as a gift – and it is. We would not make it through periods of overwhelm, stress or trauma without it. Our survival systems protect us when the world feels unsafe.

But we are not meant to live there.

We do not want our friends, our neighbours, our young people, our schools or our systems to be constantly operating in crisis. We do not want this for the greater collective. We want to lighten the load. We want to create the kind of safety that allows people to step, even briefly, into explore mode, where there is room for curiosity, connection and growth.

Trauma-informed practice is about designing our environments and shaping our relationships so that people do not have to stay in survival mode all of the time. It is about creating conditions where children, young people and adults alike can soften, breathe, and take off the armour they have had to wear for far too long.

From the village to the void

You've likely heard the common phrase, 'It takes a village to raise a child'. Somewhere along the way, many of us lost our villages.

We cannot talk about trauma without talking about the broader networks that shape our lives. When we treat trauma solely as something that lives inside individuals, we miss the social conditions that create stress, disconnection and harm in the first place.

Humans are wired to grow through connection. Yet the rise of individualism has chipped away at the support networks that once wrapped around families and communities. Where there might once have been a web of care – neighbours, grandparents, elders, aunties and uncles –there is now often one caregiver or two, doing everything behind a closed door.

In traditional cultures, caregiving is often shared. Children are seen as a collective responsibility. But in many modern Western societies, the message is that you should do it all on your own. It's families, particularly parents, who are left to carry the heaviest load. When things aren't going well, the pressure is enormous.

We see this same pattern play out in our workplaces, too. Take a teacher, for example. A teacher might be supporting a classroom full of students with complex needs, trying to teach, connect, regulate and remain calm all at once. If they are doing this in a school where staff wellbeing is not prioritised, where support is stretched, where everyone is too overwhelmed to notice how heavy the load has become, that teacher is not only isolated, they are being set up to burn out.

We have stressed-out adults trying to be regulated caregivers.

In reality, most of us are doing the best we can within the systems and societal structures in front of us.

I genuinely believe that nobody wakes up and chooses to harm someone else. But harm still happens.

Harm happens when the pressure is enormous. Harm happens when we are unwell. Harm happens when we are isolated, unsupported and carrying too much on our own. Harm happens in the void.

Trauma happens in the void.

So, let's explore what trauma is.

What is trauma?

Most of us have some idea of what trauma is, particularly what a traumatic event might look like. But even in the mid-2020s, in a world where being trauma-informed has become quite popular, we're still carrying around myths and misconceptions about what trauma is and what it is not.

For example, some people still believe that trauma in early childhood doesn't really matter because they are too young to remember it. Others might think trauma is rare, mostly only impacting people who have served in wars or experienced extreme violence.

So, let's unpack this.

Take a moment to consider:

- How do I define trauma?
- How do we talk about it in my workplace?

We might speak about trauma as an *event* or a *series of events*. But that is not entirely accurate.

Trauma is a result of being exposed to an incident, or a series of events, that are distressing, out-of-our-control and potentially life-threatening.

Trauma isn't the event itself. It's what happens inside us afterwards.

For example, you and I could both witness a distressing event. We might be standing side-by-side, watching it unfold in real time. But what happens for each of us in the days and weeks that follow could be completely different.

You might feel shaken, but return to baseline a few hours later. I, on the other hand, might have ongoing challenges. I might struggle to sleep for weeks, feeling a heightened sense of fear, and avoid heading out in public.

It's our *response* to the event. And this response isn't conscious.

It's not about weakness, or resilience, or mindset. It's the body, brain and nervous system doing what they have learned to do to keep us safe.

What do trauma responses look like?

Bessel van der Kolk, author of *The Body Keeps the Score* (2014), explains: 'These events leave us stuck in a state of helplessness and terror, and result in a change in how we perceive danger.'

Sleepless nights, racing thoughts and a constant sense of alertness are signs of a nervous system doing its best to process and protect after something has felt overwhelming. They are trauma responses.

Trauma can show up as:

- emotional responses (e.g. experiencing shock or fear)
- physical responses (e.g. headaches in the short-term, illness or inflammation in the long-term)
- changes in behaviour (e.g. avoidance or hypervigilance)
- challenges in our relationships (e.g. wanting to spend more time alone, less patience).

The word 'trauma' comes from the Greek word for 'wound'.

And what do we know about physical wounds? They show up *after* the impact. They signal that something hurt, something ruptured. They need time, space and care to heal.

And that is the good news: we can work on healing a wound.

Events cannot be healed; they cannot be undone. If trauma were just the event itself, we wouldn't be able to do much about it; we can't go back in time and undo what happened.

Trauma isn't the past. Trauma is the way it manifests in the now. When we see it as a present wound, we can start to care for it.

Not all wounds are visible. Some of us are carrying deep wounds. We might think we're covering them up, but they have their ways of showing up, eventually.

And this is where being trauma-informed begins: knowing what trauma is. Knowing we won't always see it, but choosing to show up with compassion anyway.

Childhood trauma

Childhood trauma, also called *developmental trauma*, refers to trauma that occurs during our early years. It is distinct from other types of trauma because it directly impacts how we develop. This is especially true during the earliest years of life, from birth to around age three or four, when our brains, bodies and stress-response systems are wiring up in response to the world around us.

Early childhood trauma, according to Dr Bruce Perry (2006), refers to experiences or patterns of experiences that impair a child's stress-response system, making them more reactive or sensitive. These experiences can include abuse, neglect, abandonment or significant losses such as the death of a parent.

Developmental trauma, a term closely associated with Perry's work, specifically describes the impact of repeated trauma and loss within a child's important relationships, often occurring early in life.

During our early childhood, we are learning about ourselves and the world around us. This learning is happening through our relationships with others. During this time, our caregivers, the adults we spend the most time with, are our main teachers and the architects of our world.

When we are raised by safe, loving and present caregivers, we embody powerful messages such as:

- My world is safe
- People are loving
- My needs can be met
- I am lovable
- I am worthy.

We may start to develop the template needed to spend time in 'explore mode'. We feel safe enough to be curious, playful and connected. This is what John Bowlby (1980) describes as a positive internal working model.

When we are raised in stressful environments, with caregivers who are absent or harmful, we embody messages such as:

- My world is dangerous
- People cannot be relied upon
- My needs will not be met
- I am not lovable
- I am unworthy.

In response, we begin to adapt in incredibly clever and protective ways. We don't consciously decide this, of course. But our nervous systems do it for us. Over time, we learn to stay in *survival mode*, where scanning for threats, staying guarded or staying invisible feels safer than exploring.

This is why we start to wear armour.

Studies have shown that critical periods in early development shape how the brain and autonomic nervous system respond to stress, impacting how we self-regulate for the rest of our lives. The body remembers, even when the conscious mind doesn't.

You've likely worked alongside a young person who sees the world through this survival lens. Maybe they enter a room already scanning for threats. Maybe they won't accept help, even when it's offered. Maybe they've told you they're a bad kid.

The reality is, they haven't experienced enough safe connection in those early years.

But that doesn't mean it's too late. It might be the most important part of our work – to show them, slowly and consistently, that adults can be safe. That they are worthy; they are lovable. That healing is possible.

And if you are reading this and wondering about your own early experiences, that message is for you as well. Healing is possible, and it is just as central to your work as it is to the work you do with others.

Trauma and the brain, body and nervous system

When we're working with children and young people, particularly those who've experienced trauma, it helps to know a little about how the brain and body work.

For me, learning this was a game-changer. It helped me make sense of behaviours that once felt confusing or challenging. It reminded me that what we see on the surface is often just a clue, and that curiosity and patience are some of our most important tools.

If you've ever supported a young person who seems to go from zero to 100 just like that, or who shuts down suddenly, or whose reactions feel disproportionate to the moment, this section is for you.

The brain

We don't need to be neuroscientists to be trauma-informed. But having a shared, simple way of thinking about the brain's role in stress, behaviour and learning can be incredibly helpful, particularly in trauma-affected settings.

For many years, trauma-informed practice has drawn on simple models of the brain to help explain why behaviour changes under stress. These models have been helpful in shifting shame-based narratives towards more compassionate ones.

At the same time, neuroscience continues to evolve. Contemporary research reminds us that the brain is highly interconnected, adaptive and influenced by our bodies, relationships and environments. No single part of the brain works in isolation. Thinking, feeling and survival processes are deeply interwoven rather than separate systems (Langley-Freeman et al., 2023).

With that in mind, the following explanation of the brain, alongside figure 4, overleaf, can help us make sense of why people sometimes struggle to think, regulate or engage under stress.

A widely accepted view is that the brain develops from the bottom up. This means the systems that support survival and protection develop first, and the systems that support reflection, planning and reasoning develop later (Siegel, 2012).

At the base of the brain is the brain stem. This area helps regulate essential survival functions such as breathing, heart rate and digestion. It also plays a central role in our stress responses. When we perceive danger, the brain

Figure 4: The brain

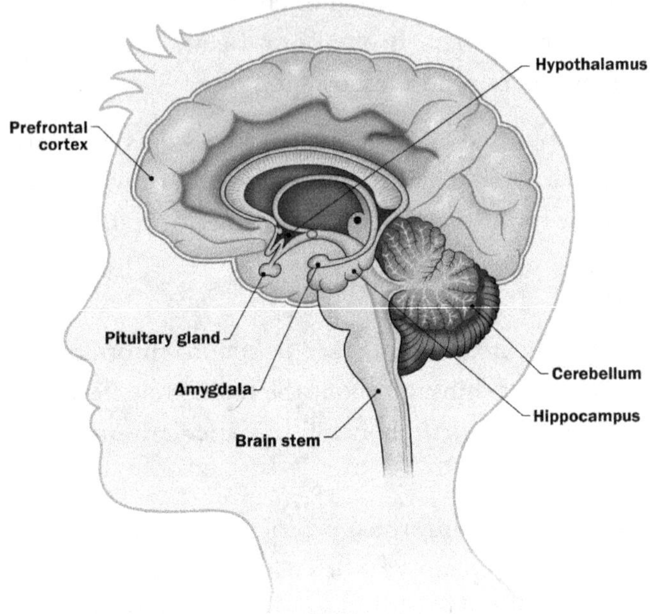

stem helps mobilise the body to respond quickly, preparing us to fight, flee, freeze or shut down – often before we have consciously processed what is happening (Perry & Szalavitz, 2017).

Sitting above this is the limbic system, a network involved in emotion, memory, attachment and connection. Within this system is the amygdala, often described as the brain's alarm system. The amygdala is constantly scanning for threat and responds rapidly. This is why feelings such as fear, anger or anxiety can arise before we have had time to make sense of a situation. These responses are fast because they are designed to protect us.

At the front of the brain is the prefrontal cortex. This part of the brain supports planning, problem-solving, impulse control, perspective-taking and decision-making. It continues to develop into early adulthood and is particularly sensitive to stress. When we are overwhelmed or feeling unsafe, access to these reflective capacities is reduced (Siegel, 2012).

Importantly, these reflective capacities are the most vulnerable under stress. When we feel overwhelmed, unsafe or under sustained pressure, access to reflection, learning and flexible thinking can reduce significantly. This is because our system is prioritising survival and keeping us safe.

That's not bad behaviour. That's biology, shaped by stress, experience and context.

The body

The brain doesn't act alone. Trauma also shows up in the body: in the way we hold ourselves, how we breathe, how our muscles tense, how our stomach aches or how our heart races. This is because the brain and body are connected by the nervous system.

The autonomic nervous system has two main branches:

- The sympathetic nervous system gets us ready to act. It's responsible for that surge of energy we feel when we're anxious or scared, increasing heart rate, dilating pupils and sending blood to the muscles. This is the part that powers fight or flight.
- The parasympathetic nervous system helps us rest and recover. It slows our breathing, lowers our heart rate and allows us to digest, connect and heal.

When we grow up in a consistently safe and supportive environment, our nervous system learns how to move between these states as needed. But when we grow up around chronic stress or trauma, our nervous system may get stuck in high alert, always prepared for danger, even when no threat is present.

For those of us working in complex settings, we might see this every day. A child who can't sit still. A student who lashes out. A colleague who seems constantly on edge.

Or we might feel it in ourselves. Irritable, exhausted or unable to rest. This is the nervous system at work. And it's why trauma-informed practice needs to include not just our minds, but our bodies too.

Stress or trauma?

Not everything stressful is trauma. But trauma is *always* overwhelmingly and undeniably stressful.

You might like to read that again.

Put simply, stress is a physical and psychological reaction to a demand, or stressor.

Some stress helps us grow. We call this positive stress, like the nerves before a big presentation or the challenge of learning to drive a car. When we have support and the stress is short-lived, it can build resilience. The end result might be a new skill or a positive outcome, like getting a good grade or earning your driver's licence.

Tolerable stress is more serious, such as going through grief or experiencing a major life change (e.g. a family separation). With supportive relationships, we recover and we might even find meaning through these experiences.

Toxic stress is different. It's intense, ongoing and happens without the buffer of safe, supportive relationships. This is where trauma often lives.

Imagine a child who experiences violence at home, and no one notices. Or a young person who is constantly moved from one placement to another, never knowing whom they can trust. Or a staff member who is exposed to others' trauma day in and day out without time to process or rest.

When stress becomes chronic and there is no chance to recover, it starts to take a toll on our brain, our body and other aspects of our lives.

People who've adapted to high-stress environments often look like they're coping just fine. But inside, they're surviving, not thriving.

We are living in a time when the word 'trauma' gets used to describe anything and everything uncomfortable. It's well-intentioned. But sometimes, we call stress trauma when it's not. And sometimes, in our efforts to protect others, especially children, from *any* form of stress, we lose those growth opportunities.

For stress to be positive or tolerable, we need buffers. We need care, community and opportunities to rest and repair.

The four Fs of survival: fight, flight, freeze and fawn

A few nights ago, I woke at 3am to the sound of glass shattering in my kitchen.

Startled, I sat up, only to hear it again.

Without thinking, I jumped out of bed and dashed towards the noise. I didn't take my phone, nor did I grab anything to defend myself; I just ran straight into the unknown.

When I got to the kitchen, I found a cat – not even my cat, but a neighbour's. It sat by a smashed olive oil bottle, meowing at the door to be let out. How it had entered my apartment and stayed unnoticed until 3am I'll never know.

What I do know is that my stress response was in full gear, pushing me into a fight reaction. My brain and body had switched into survival mode. The sound of shattering glass triggered my amygdala which overrode rational thought and problem-solving in favour of action. My heart raced, my shoulders tensed and sweat began to form in my palms.

It took me a long time to get back into a restful sleep.

When the brain and body perceive a threat, whether it's real or imagined, our nervous system kicks into gear. These responses are not conscious choices. They are automatic. Instinctive. Designed to keep us alive.

Take a moment and think of a time you perceived a threat or faced a dangerous situation. What happened inside your body? How did you behave?

In trauma-informed work, we often talk about four primary survival responses: fight, flight, freeze and fawn. Let's take my example with the smashing glass and compare the ways I could have reacted. I could have gone into:

- flight mode, and run from the sound
- freeze mode, and hidden under the covers in my bed
- fawn mode, and prepared to comply with the intruder to avoid escalation.

Each of these reactions serves as a protective mechanism in the moment.

But trauma will have us existing in these states in more ongoing and exhaustive ways.

Let's consider how these responses might show up in young people, ourselves and our colleagues. It is, of course, different for everyone, and table 1 serves as a guide, not a prescription.

Table 1: Fight, flight, freeze and fawn

Response	Possible body sensations	Behaviours in young people	Behaviours in adults and colleagues
Fight	Tense muscles Clenched jaw or fists Heat rising Rapid heartbeat	Aggression, yelling Hitting, kicking, throwing Talking back or challenging authority	Snapping in meetings Overcontrolling Quick to anger or criticism Defensive posture or tone
Flight	Restless legs Butterflies in stomach Racing thoughts Feeling jittery or on edge	Running away Avoiding eye contact or certain spaces Repeatedly asking to leave Fidgeting or pacing	Avoiding tasks or conversations Always 'busy' or over-scheduled Withdrawing from the team
Freeze	Numbness Heavy body Shallow breathing Blank or foggy feeling	Staring into space Not responding when spoken to Seeming 'frozen' or absent Refusing to engage	Procrastinating Zoning out during conversations Feeling stuck or paralysed Appearing disengaged Scrolling phone during meetings
Fawn	Shallow breathing Inner tension Nervous smile Tight chest	People-pleasing Always trying to help adults Fear of getting into trouble Over-apologising	Overcommitting or saying yes to everything Avoiding conflict at all costs Prioritising others' needs over their own Agreeable to keep the peace

Being trauma-informed invites curiosity. We move away from 'What's wrong with them?' and towards 'What might this be protecting them from?', 'I wonder what sensations they're experiencing right now?', or, even better, 'I wonder what might help them feel safer?'

This lens matters.

It's what turns schools and organisations into safer spaces – for young people, yes, but also for ourselves. Because the more we understand these responses in one another, the more we can offer compassion, not correction. Boundaries, not blame. Support, not shame.

Chapter summary

- Trauma isn't the event itself; it's what happens inside us afterwards. It lives in the body, the brain and the nervous system.
- Our culture of individualism has stripped away the village that once wrapped around people. Many of us are trying to survive with too little support.
- Survival mode is not a personal failure, but a protective state, characterised by the four Fs: fight, flight, freeze and fawn.
- Individual trauma is shaped by collective conditions. Stress, disconnection and harm often reflect broader social systems.
- Childhood trauma affects how we grow, relate and regulate. It shapes the foundations of our nervous systems and our sense of self.
- Being trauma-informed means knowing we won't always see someone's wounds, but choosing to show up with compassion anyway.

From insight to impact

- **Reflect on survival mode.** Can you identify a time when you or your workplace have been operating in survival mode? What did it feel like? What helped you navigate this period?
- **Contribute to the village.** Ask: do we have a strong village? Is it inclusive? How can we restore connection, collective care or shared responsibility in small but meaningful ways? You might start with a conversation with someone new.

- **Start with compassion.** We won't always know who is carrying trauma, but we can choose to respond with kindness, not judgement. Use this chapter to open up conversations about what trauma-informed relationships and environments might look like where you are.

3

Running the Relay: Carrying Other People's Trauma

We've all heard the saying 'it's a marathon, not a sprint'. It's often used to describe the long game of working in helping professions. It's meant to reassure us, permitting us to take our time with the work.

But I've been wondering whether this metaphor is actually harming our wellbeing. Have you ever run a marathon? It's pretty exhausting. It's a solo pursuit. It often ends in collapse. It assumes you'll keep going until you've got nothing left.

I once ran a half-marathon that ended with fewer toenails than when I began (sorry, but it's true)! It was pretty painful, and the recovery took a little while. I enjoyed it, but there is no way I could do that every single day.

Recently, I came across a far better metaphor for those of us in the helping professions. Dr Rola Hallam, a Syrian doctor and humanitarian, spoke at the 2024 Trauma and Mental Health Masters event in Oxford. She said, 'It's not a marathon, it's a relay.'

She was speaking about trauma work and the weight of responsibility we carry in spaces marked by suffering, complexity and systemic harm. Her message was clear: the work is far too heavy for any one person to hold alone. The truth of her words applies powerfully to education, caring roles and youth support.

A relay is something I can get behind. I carry the baton for a while, and then I pass it to someone else. I rest. I take care of myself. Maybe I even have some fun in between legs. And when I'm ready, I'll pick up the baton again.

The baton itself becomes symbolic, too. Once I've passed it on, I don't need to feel its weight anymore. I don't need to take it home with me. Somebody else is taking care of it.

Educating young people and walking alongside our youth isn't about endless self-sacrifice. It asks us to notice when we're pouring from an empty cup, and to be honest about what it might take to refill it – or, at the very least, to keep it from running dry.

Sustainable care, whether for students, clients or our own families, can't come from exhaustion.

It comes from rhythms that allow us to rest and return. From shared responsibility. From cultures where it is safe to say 'I need support' without fear or shame.

The relay matters because it reminds us that this work was never meant to be carried by one person, or even one role. When we honour that, we stop confusing endurance with care. We stop praising self-sacrifice and start protecting capacity.

And slowly, the weight shifts. Wellbeing becomes something we build together, not something individuals are expected to manufacture on their own.

How we're exposed to other people's trauma

When we work with someone who has experienced trauma, it is possible that we will feel some of the weight of their experiences ourselves.

Many people working in schools and complex settings develop refined coping and wellbeing strategies that support them to manage this exposure while being effective in their work. Others, like me as a graduate, hide the impact and slowly become desensitised.

There are real risks in trauma-impacted settings, and we need to name them if we want to manage them openly and sustainably.

We can be exposed to others' trauma by:

- directly witnessing an event
- being a first responder
- receiving a disclosure
- viewing distressing content
- responding to dysregulated behaviour
- seeing harm unfold and feeling powerless to change it.

We are also impacted by the injustices we witness in systems and structures, and by the ongoing emotional labour of holding space for other people's pain.

In May 2025, the Australian media highlighted findings from Deakin University that educators experience secondary traumatic stress at higher levels than paramedics and other health professionals (Fraser & Molineux, 2025).

What the media headlines largely skipped were the helpful recommendations which included formally recognising risk for educators, implementing trauma-informed practice in schools, and coordinating more effectively between schools and community services, to name a few.

I support bringing the reality of traumatic stress to the surface because it reflects what people are actually living, and because it helps us see where care, protection and support are most urgently needed.

We need to talk about it. We know that ongoing exposure to trauma can lead to compassion fatigue, vicarious trauma and burnout. These impacts are often cumulative, building quietly over time.

This chapter gives us permission to pause, to name the cost without judgement, and to normalise the need for care. Along the way, we'll explore ways to notice warning signs, ground ourselves and build cultures where conversations about wellbeing are welcomed rather than avoided.

Vicarious trauma and a shift in world view

It's no surprise that trauma-impacted work impacts us.

In the literature, this impact is described using terms such as 'vicarious trauma' and 'compassion fatigue'. Some researchers draw distinctions between them; others use the terms interchangeably. In practice, they tend to travel together. They describe overlapping ways the cost of caring shows up when exposure is ongoing and support is insufficient.

Vicarious trauma is an occupational risk for people working alongside children and young people, arising from repeated exposure to others' traumatic experiences. The impact of witnessing other people's trauma is not limited to our emotions. Research shows it can affect our mental health, physical wellbeing, relationships, sense of meaning and capacity to function at work (Bride, 2007).

At its core, vicarious trauma is a shift in world view after exposure to someone else's trauma. It can lead us to experience similar reactions to those who directly experience the trauma. You might notice yourself feeling triggered, fearful or dysregulated when confronted by reminders of what you've been exposed to. For example:

- A peer support worker hears many accounts of suicide attempts and they begin to feel hopeless about recovery, despite previously feeling optimistic in their own journey.
- A foster carer develops hypervigilance, worried they can never predict the next outburst from the child in their care. They feel desperate to learn every detail of the child's history in the hope of avoiding triggers.
- A youth worker supporting several young people who have been physically abused starts having recurring dreams about children being harmed, and feels a heightened protectiveness towards all children they meet.

The neurobiology behind vicarious trauma functions in much the same way as first-hand trauma: our brain and body are trying to keep us safe and help us survive. Serious exposure to others' trauma without protective mechanisms places any of us at risk.

Just as trauma shows up differently for every person, so too do the impacts of vicarious trauma. Some people may feel emotionally numb or shut down, while others become highly reactive or hypervigilant.

Arthurson, Lohmeyer and Riggs (2025) found that exposure to trauma-impacted work can evoke a range of responses, including:

- difficulty managing emotions, or feeling persistently on edge
- fatigue, poor sleep, or physical complaints such as headaches, stomach upset, or frequent illness
- trouble concentrating or feeling easily distracted, which can increase the risk of mistakes or accidents
- loss of meaning or hope, or feeling the world is unsafe
- withdrawal from friends, family, or intimacy, or conversely, conflict and irritability in relationships
- increased reliance on unhelpful coping strategies such as overeating, substance use, or risky behaviours
- avoiding certain work tasks or even avoiding clients altogether
- in more serious cases, symptoms resemble post-traumatic stress disorder.

This list is not exhaustive. Recognising this diversity of reactions is vital, because it helps reduce shame and opens the door for more compassionate, tailored approaches to support and recovery.

Sometimes, the impact doesn't show up as something dramatic or obvious. Sometimes, it arrives in much smaller, more ordinary moments.

The cheese toastie meltdown

Have you had a cheese toastie meltdown?

If you work in an alternative school or the out-of-home-care youth sector, you'll probably relate. Maybe the image of the cheese toastie has already triggered something inside of you.

A cheese toastie meltdown is a hard-hitting moment when you feel you've got nothing left to give. A young person urgently asks you to make them a toastie while you're frantically juggling heavy disclosures, case notes and concerns over the safety of another young person.

And suddenly, something inside you tightens. The request feels irritating. You struggle to empathise with this young person in front of you (who likely hasn't eaten overnight, or hasn't had an adult acknowledge them yet today, and is really just asking to have their needs met).

You eventually catch yourself, realising you're exhausted, and wonder where all your empathy has gone.

This is the epitome of compassion fatigue.

Compassion fatigue is the emotional toll of caring for others when you haven't been able to refuel, recharge and care for yourself, or allow others to care for you (Figley, 2002; Maté, 2021).

You may experience some telling signs, such as:

- feeling detached or hopeless
- isolating yourself from others
- a lack of interest in everyday tasks and hobbies
- feeling drained, physically or mentally
- neglecting your own needs
- physical symptoms, including headaches, changes to your eating habits, difficulty sleeping or excessive sleeping.

The good (and maybe surprising) news is that compassion itself didn't cause the fatigue. You can't run out of compassion. It can certainly feel that way at the time, but compassion is not a finite resource that suddenly empties.

Being in roles that allow us to express our compassion and help others can be meaningful and fulfilling. We're naturally compassionate beings; it isn't compassion that drains us, it's withholding compassion from ourselves. We try to fix the unfixable or manage the unmanageable – and then turn on ourselves when we can't (Maté, 2021). Harsh self-talk, blame and 'I should have done more' creep in, even when 'more' was impossible.

That's a pretty harsh way to be with ourselves.

When we work in these caring roles, our relationships are often what I call one-way compassionate. The child or young person can't (and shouldn't have to) offer equal compassion back. That imbalance is inherent in the work.

Which is exactly why compassion must also flow inwards, and be held collectively by teams, leaders, and systems.

When compassion only ever moves outwards, fatigue inevitably follows.

But for many people working in trauma-affected settings, fatigue is only part of the story. There is another layer of distress that sits beneath exhaustion – one that has far less to do with individual coping and far more to do with the systems we are working within.

This is the distress that comes from knowing what a child, young person, or family needs, and being unable to provide it.

This is where we begin to talk about moral injury.

Moral injury

Moral injury describes the distress we feel when we are unable to act in line with our values, or when we witness or participate in something that goes against what we believe is right (Litz et al., 2009; Griffin et al., 2019).

Unlike trauma that stems from threats to safety, moral injury centres on violations of what we hold to be moral, ethical or just. It is not as widely researched as vicarious trauma or compassion fatigue, but it is increasingly recognised as a significant risk for professionals working with children and young people (Williamson et al., 2018).

When we experience moral injury, it can be because we've made decisions that go against our own values, or because we're operating within rigid systems that we know may be harming the very people we are there to protect.

For example:

- A workplace may exclude a young person for 'acting out' when we know exclusion only deepens harm.
- A child protection worker may be forced by protocol to make a placement decision that they know isn't the best option for the child.
- A teacher may see systemic racism impacting their students and feel powerless to intervene.

That is where moral injury happens: when great practitioners find themselves compromising their values, where the systems around them are not yet aligned with trauma-informed ways of working.

At the heart of trauma-informed practice is unconditional positive regard: the belief that young people do well when they can, and that behaviour should never define a person's worth. Many practitioners naturally gravitate towards this stance. Yet too often, our policies, procedures and performance measures pull us in the opposite direction.

Moral injury does not look the same for everyone. For some, it manifests as guilt, shame or hopelessness. For others, it is anger at colleagues or institutions.

It may show up as:

- persistent self-blame or guilt
- withdrawal, isolation or disillusionment
- a loss of meaning or trust in institutions
- anger, betrayal, or cynicism about the system
- avoidance of certain tasks or even entire roles
- a loss of faith in one's capacity to make a difference.

These reactions can be deeply unsettling because they cut to the core of why people enter caring professions in the first place. As Griffin et al. (2019) note, moral injury is about betrayal and broken trust.

To truly prevent moral injury, we need more than individual coping strategies. It is neither fair nor effective to leave this burden with individuals who are trying to 'hold the line' on trauma-informed practice in isolation. We need leaders and whole-organisation systems that create the conditions for values and practice to align.

Trauma-informed practice gives us a lens for making human-centred decisions, preventing re-traumatisation and putting compassion into action – not just for our students, but for ourselves and our colleagues.

Running the relay – here's what we can do

I've had my own cheese toastie meltdowns. I've blurred boundaries because I cared. I've lain awake at night catastrophising, only to realise the next morning that I was carrying a baton that was never mine to hold.

That's the thing about this work. When you care deeply, it's very easy to start running legs of the relay that don't belong to you.

But trauma-informed practice asks something different of us. It asks us to care with awareness, not self-erasure. It asks us to protect our capacity so we can stay steady, present and human for the long haul.

Working in trauma-impacted settings means we are exposed, emotionally, relationally and morally. We cannot eliminate that exposure. What we *can* do is become more intentional about how we respond to it, individually and collectively.

One framework I've found helpful, both in the research and in practice, is the ABC model of vicarious trauma prevention: awareness, balance and connection (Saakvitne & Pearlman, 1996).

Awareness

Awareness is about noticing how the work impacts us, both in the moment and over time. This means tuning in to our stress responses, paying attention to the signals our body is giving us and being honest about how we're coping.

Awareness might come through mindfulness, journalling, regulation strategies, peer support or speaking to a trusted professional.

It also means reflecting on our own stories. Our childhood experiences and personal histories shape how we show up with young people. For some of us, certain behaviours or disclosures will hit closer to home. Knowing this doesn't disqualify us from the work; it helps us anticipate what might be hard, where we may need extra support, and what unique empathy and strengths we bring because of those experiences.

Balance

Balance reminds us that our lives can't be consumed entirely by the work. We need to keep engaging with hobbies, interests and relationships that remind us we are whole people outside of our roles.

This is about finding a rhythm between work, play and rest, rather than swinging between over-functioning and collapse.

Connection

Connection is the third part of the model, and it may be the most powerful of all. We need connection with ourselves, with others and with a broader sense of meaning and purpose.

All the wellbeing research points to relationships with others as one of the strongest predictors of resilience and recovery. When we intentionally invest in the people who care for us, both inside and outside of work, we create networks that buffer us against stress. Connection is about giving, but it's also about allowing ourselves to receive, letting others step in when we need to rest. It's a theme we'll return to throughout this book.

These three elements are things we can take personal responsibility for, but they do not exist in a vacuum. They are practices we can each build into our lives. But they become even more effective in trauma-informed workplaces that understand the risks, normalise these conversations and actively create cultures where they are supported.

Accepting support comes easier when leaders offer it. Boundaries are easier to hold when they are respected. Connection is easier to foster when workplaces make time and space for it. The ABCs are most protective when they are not just individual habits but part of the wider system we are working in.

What follows are not rules or checklists, but practical ways many of us learn to protect our capacity over time. They are small, intentional practices that help us stay in the work without losing ourselves to it.

Setting boundaries

Boundaries are one of the most protective practices we have in trauma-impacted work, and often one of the hardest to hold.

It can be helpful to pause and ask ourselves some very practical questions:

- What is my role?
- What hours do I work?
- I will support a child or young person when:
- I will refer on to another service when:
- Are these boundaries clear to my students, clients and colleagues?

When we care deeply, it's easy to blur professional boundaries or stretch ourselves beyond our role because we want to help. We may also be working in cultures that quietly reward long hours, constant availability and going above and beyond, even when it comes at a cost.

But boundaries are not barriers. They are what allow us to show up stronger and for longer.

Clear boundaries give children and young people predictability and safety. They help others understand what we can offer and when. And they protect our capacity to keep offering care without burning out.

Being clear about your role, your hours and the limits of your support takes practice. It can be helpful to work through this with a mentor, supervisor or trusted colleague, particularly if boundaries have been hard for you to hold in the past.

Ending the day: leaving the baton behind

One weekend, a teacher rang me in tears about a young person in crisis. You know that awful mix of love, fear and responsibility that has you ruminating? Well, this time, it was disrupting her sleep.

We sat on the phone and walked through our professional checklist together:

- Had we spoken with him and his caregivers? Yes.
- Safety plan in place? Yes.
- Referrals made? Yes.

- Notes completed and relevant agencies notified? Yes.
- An on-call pathway for emergencies? Yes.

We had passed the baton for the weekend. Someone else was holding it now.

That clarity didn't erase the concern, but it gave her permission to sleep, to protect her nervous system. On Monday, we'd be there on the track, ready to pick up the baton again and run our leg with the young person.

Boundaries aren't about caring less; they're about caring sustainably. They help us think more clearly, rest more fully and rarely regret the decisions we make.

Using an end-of-day checklist can help us move from looping worry to grounded clarity. It allows us to systematically review what needs to be done, but also to acknowledge what we have already done. This simple practice can reduce rumination after hours and support better psychological separation between work and rest.

Your checklist might include things like:

- having a check-in conversation with the child or young person
- scheduling a care team meeting
- contacting a parent or guardian
- making a referral to a service
- seeking guidance from a leader
- making a child protection report
- completing case notes
- developing or updating a safety plan.

Once you have compiled a list, take a look and ask yourself:

Have I done everything I can, within my role, today?

Often, the answer is yes – and further worry won't change the outcome.

If the answer is no, the checklist gives you clarity about the next step to take during work hours, rather than carrying it into the night.

Once you have created a list like this, you can keep it and use it next time you're supporting a young person through a challenging experience or when you're feeling overwhelmed.

Developing an end-of-day ritual

In trauma-impacted work, we need ways to mark the transition between professional time and personal time. Rituals help signal to our nervous system that the work has paused.

During the long Melbourne lockdowns, I became very intentional about my end-of-day rituals. I was working from a tiny one-bedroom apartment, so the boundaries between work and life blurred quickly. And, in that period of time, the team I was leading made a record number of child protection reports. It felt like we were experiencing one crisis after another.

At first, the heaviness of the job seemed to creep through my apartment. Eventually, I created a simple ritual: packing away my work materials, changing out of my work clothes (yes, I still wore them at home) and stepping outside for fresh air and movement.

It wasn't perfect. It took practice. But over time, these small actions helped me hold boundaries, compartmentalise the day, and symbolically mark where my leg of the relay ended.

You can create your own version of this ritual. It doesn't have to be elaborate; it just has to signal to your brain and body: *the baton is down and work is done for now.*

Examples of end-of-day rituals include:

- a check-out question or short chat with colleagues
- journalling: *what went well today (and why)?*
- turning off work devices
- removing work clothes
- washing the day away with a shower or swim
- stepping outside
- gentle or energising movement
- socialising with people who fill you up
- choosing a cut-off time for work talk
- playing a particular 'work is done' song.

What would you add to the list?

Self-compassion: treating yourself like your best friend

If you've chosen to work with children and young people, you're already practising compassion every day. You notice suffering, you feel for the human experience in front of you, and you respond with warmth and care. Self-compassion is no different, except the someone who needs recognition and kindness is you.

Kristin Neff, the leading researcher on self-compassion, describes it as the simple but radical act of turning the qualities we extend to others – care, empathy and understanding – towards ourselves (Neff, 2003; Neff & Germer, 2017).

She explains that self-compassion has three components:

- **Mindfulness:** the ability to bring gentle awareness to what we are experiencing without exaggerating or minimising it.
- **Common humanity:** remembering that struggle is part of being human and that others in our position would also find it difficult.
- **Self-kindness:** treating ourselves with the same care and encouragement we would offer a dear friend.

Self-compassion isn't a fixed trait that some people are born with; it's a skill to be practised. This is not always easy work, but not doing it makes everything harder.

I know this well. As a school leader, I held expectations of myself that I would never expect of anyone else. When I didn't meet them, I criticised myself relentlessly. It was exhausting.

I still catch myself doing this now, even as I write this book.

Sometimes the practice is as small as noticing the inner critic and shifting the tone. Sometimes it is pausing to say, 'This is hard, and anyone in my shoes would find it hard. What do I need right now?'

Other times it is deliberately engaging in more structured practices, such as guided self-compassion meditations, journalling, intentional breaks or self-compassionate touch.

I highly recommend checking out the free resources and practices that Kristin Neff shares on self-compassion, which can be found at self-compassion.org.

The benefits of supporting people impacted by trauma

This chapter may have felt weighted towards the risks and challenges of our work, and those risks are very real. But hopefully, some of the strategies outlined so far have also offered reassurance – that there are ways to keep showing up with energy and passion.

We've spent time exploring what happens when we are exposed to other people's trauma, but there's a much less talked-about story, too: the possibility of growth that can come from working alongside people who have experienced trauma.

These experiences are known as secondary post-traumatic growth or vicarious post-traumatic growth.

To build our understanding, let's first look at post-traumatic growth.

Post-traumatic growth

Post-traumatic growth is the positive psychological change that some individuals experience after a life crisis or traumatic event.

Richard Tedeschi and Lawrence Calhoun researched experiences of post-traumatic growth in the 1990s and described five categories of growth:

1. the ability to recognise and embrace new opportunities
2. stronger relationships with loved ones as well as with victims who suffered in the same way
3. cultivation of inner strength through the knowledge that they have overcome tremendous hardship
4. a deeper appreciation for life
5. a changing and evolving relationship to religion and spirituality.

Importantly, this growth can exist alongside stress and struggle; it isn't about erasing pain. But it does show that new meaning can come from difficulty.

Research has found post-traumatic growth is associated with greater life satisfaction (Mols et al., 2009), happiness (Lelorain et al., 2010), and overall psychological, physical and emotional wellbeing (Wild & Paivio, 2003).

Secondary (vicarious) post-traumatic growth

The same is true for those of us supporting others. Just as we can be negatively affected by trauma exposure, we can also experience secondary post-traumatic growth.

Manning-Jones, de Terte, and Stephens (2015), in a review of 28 studies, found that professionals in trauma-exposed work reported many of the same types of growth: spiritual growth, inner strength and stronger relationships. Many also spoke about the deep sense of meaning that came from knowing they were making a difference in the lives of people who had experienced trauma.

So what helps facilitate this growth? The literature points to qualities such as optimism, empathy and competence in our roles. This makes sense. When we feel resourced, skilled and able to connect meaningfully, the work doesn't just drain us, it can enrich us. Other factors include some of the strategies we've already talked about: the ABC model for preventing vicarious trauma, supportive peer relationships (one of my favourite findings), and a strong commitment to self-care practices.

This is heartening. It means the same conditions that protect us from harm are also the conditions that open the door to growth.

As we move through the next chapters together, we'll keep building on these practices. We'll explore how to boost optimism, build competence, strengthen peer support and deepen our care for ourselves and each other. Because while this work will always carry weight, it can also be a source of meaning, connection and even transformation.

Chapter summary

- Working in trauma-impacted settings can expose us to others' trauma through direct incidents, disclosures, distressing content, systemic injustice and the ongoing emotional labour of holding space for others.
- Compassion fatigue is not caused by compassion itself, but by giving without replenishment, blurred boundaries and a lack of self-compassion.
- Risks such as vicarious trauma, moral injury and burnout can be reduced through proactive strategies such as clear boundaries, intentional end-of-day rituals, peer connection and self-compassion practices.
- Trauma-informed practice protects both staff and those we support by creating environments that are safe, connected and values-aligned.
- Alongside the risks, there is potential for secondary post-traumatic growth – finding meaning, purpose and personal growth through supporting others impacted by trauma.

From insight to impact

- **Map your protective practices.** Identify which of the ABC strategies (awareness, balance, connection) you already use, and where there are gaps.
- **Normalise the relay.** Create team agreements that encourage sharing the load, taking breaks and stepping back without shame.
- **End the day intentionally.** Create your own end-of-day checklist and choose an end-of-day ritual to help you protect your personal time.
- **Invest in peer support.** Build regular spaces for colleagues to debrief, reflect and celebrate growth together.

Part II

Embed

embed *verb*
to make something an integral part of.

Merriam-Webster

We embed trauma-informed practice at every level of our work. This includes staff culture, leadership practices, workplace structures and the ways we respond to one another. We intentionally build safety, trust and empowerment, not only for the people accessing our services, but for those delivering them.

4

Building Safety: Trust, Transparency and Peer Support

Trauma-informed practice isn't something we can tick off after a one-day training or with an online certificate. It's not simply a behaviour-management strategy or a toolkit we pull out only when working with young people. If we want to create real, lasting change, it requires something deeper.

This section, Embed, is where we move beyond awareness into integration. We'll explore how trauma-informed principles come to life in practice, not just for those in our care, but across the whole community. That means looking at ourselves, our teams, our policies and the broader systems we are part of.

That means we're zooming out.

To truly embed this work, we need to weave the core principles into the fabric of our everyday environments.

This is the shift from knowing to doing, and from doing to being.

Defining trauma-informed practice

With the growing popularity of trauma-informed approaches, there is currently a bit of mess in the way it is defined and applied. When something is developing and being adopted so quickly, working definitions tend to shift just as rapidly.

That's not always a bad thing; it means we're responding to context, learning from experience and adjusting along the way.

As we touched on earlier in the book, trauma-informed practice requires that we:

- **realise** how trauma shapes individuals, groups and communities
- **recognise** the signs, symptoms and wide-reaching impacts
- **respond** in ways that meet people's needs and promote healing
- **prevent** further harm or re-traumatisation (SAMHSA, 2014).

Trauma-informed practice offers both interventions and an organisational approach. It asks us to pay attention to how we treat ourselves, how we treat one another, and how our systems either support or undermine that care. It's both responsive and proactive.

At its core, I describe trauma-informed practice as *putting compassion into action*. It's about creating environments of safety, where we prevent harm, enhance belonging and promote healing for all. That means it's about us, too.

Trauma-informed practice asks us to look not only at how we support others, but at the cultures and systems we're part of – the places where we work, learn and lead.

If we want trauma-informed schools, services and communities, we have to start by noticing what we're already reinforcing, and what we're willing to do differently. And that work starts with us.

The trauma-informed principles

One of the most widely used and internationally recognised trauma-informed frameworks comes from the Substance Abuse and Mental Health Services Administration in the United States (SAMHSA, 2014).

SAMHSA outlined a set of trauma-informed principles that help guide how individuals, teams, organisations and systems can reduce harm and promote healing. The principles are:

1. Safety
2. Trustworthiness and transparency
3. Peer support
4. Collaboration and mutuality
5. Empowerment, voice and choice
6. Cultural, historical and gender humility and responsiveness.

These principles are most often used to reflect on how we work with children, young people, clients and families who have experienced trauma. They've been adapted across education, health, community and care settings.

And, as we'll explore in this section, they also offer a powerful lens for reflecting on our own wellbeing, our relationships with colleagues, and the cultures and systems we work within.

Offering safety requires us to feel safe first

If you've ever felt frustrated during trauma-informed training, you're not alone. I hear this often.

Maybe a well-meaning consultant told you that your school's behaviour policies clash with trauma-informed principles, but didn't offer guidance on bridging that gap.

Maybe you're supporting a young person whose behaviour is so complex, so relentless, that it's left you exhausted, or even feeling unsafe. And then you're reminded your job is to help *them* feel safe, without any acknowledgement of your experience.

Maybe the training focused heavily on abuse, neglect and violence, leaving you overwhelmed, dysregulated or carrying more than you arrived with.

Or maybe child safety compliance has become so rigid that the fear of getting it wrong has created a new lack of safety.

I know these things happen, and it doesn't exactly make any of us feel safer, right? And the irony is that its not going to be making the young people feel safer, either. They're looking to us for cues of safety. What can we give them when we're showing up dysregulated and hypervigilant, too?

Trauma and toxic stress strip away safety, our sense of choice, control, trust and connection.

Being trauma-informed means we consciously and continuously rebuild it.

And that work cannot happen at a single level; it must happen across all levels of our organisations and schools. We cannot expect trauma-informed environments for young people while ignoring the safety of the adults within them. Safety is the cornerstone of trauma-informed practice, and it's complex and messy.

This work lives in duality. We can hold the responsibility of helping young people feel safe, while navigating moments when we feel stressed or need extra support. We can work on building calm, regulating environments, while we need some co-regulation from our peers. We can show up with compassion, even when we're tired or uncertain. We can commit to learning and developing skills, while supporting the young people who are learning and developing skills alongside us.

Working in a trauma-informed way will never be perfect. It's about promoting safety, again and again, and holding space for the messy, real, human parts of this work.

Across the next two chapters, we'll unpack each of the trauma-informed principles and explore how we might embed them within our personal practices, alongside our teams and within the communities we are a part of.

As we unpack each principle, taking some notes and engaging in reflection can be helpful.

You may like to consider:

- What feels strong already?
- Where do we need to grow?
- What risks or pressures do we need to name and mitigate?

Principle 1: Safety

What is it?

When I talk about safety in trauma-informed practice, I'm talking about how safety is *experienced* by the people who move through our schools and organisations each day. At its core, the goal is this:

> Members of our team, children, young people and community members feel physically, emotionally and psychologically safe. The setting and interpersonal interactions promote safety for all.

When we think about physical safety, we're ensuring that our environment, resources and expectations align with the realities of the work. This means the physical spaces, the demands of the role and the challenges we face are all supported by adequate preparation, staffing and competence.

When we think about emotional safety, we're creating spaces where people can acknowledge and process how they feel, especially in emotionally intense work. Big feelings are part of this profession. Emotional safety means people can express those feelings without fear of being judged, dismissed or penalised.

Psychological safety refers to a culture where people feel secure taking interpersonal risks, asking questions, admitting mistakes, offering ideas and speaking honestly, without fear of punishment or humiliation (Edmondson, 1999).

Why is it important?

When we experience trauma, we experience events that overwhelm our sense of control and result in a profound loss of safety. In these moments, our stress responses activate to protect us. This is adaptive and necessary in genuinely dangerous situations.

But our workplaces and organisations should not function as chronic threat environments. They should be places where safety is a priority, is promoted, and is restored quickly when challenges occur.

When safety isn't established and proactively cared for, we might notice ourselves and our colleagues slipping back into survival mode.

How do we embed the principle of safety?

Safety becomes everybody's responsibility; it's not something anyone else can promise us, it's a commitment we need to make together.

No leader, teacher or practitioner can guarantee that nothing uncomfortable will ever happen. We cannot promise that hard conversations won't arise, that emotions won't surface, or that someone won't say something that lands badly. What we *can* do is be intentional about how we prepare for these moments, how we respond when they occur, and how we repair when safety is disrupted.

I often explain this when I'm facilitating professional learning, but the same principle applies in schools, teams and organisations.

I can't promise a space will feel safe for everyone at all times. But I can name that safety matters. I can invite people into shared responsibility. I can ask what they need from me, from themselves and from each other to feel supported. And I can be prepared to respond when something doesn't go as planned.

It's not a foolproof solution, but it acknowledges the shared responsibility we all hold when we come together, and that safety takes consideration from moment to moment.

When teams understand that safety is something we actively create together, rather than something we passively expect from others, safety becomes more possible, even in complex, high-pressure environments.

Let's look at some strategies to build safety in our teams and workplace culture.

Explicitly establishing agreed ways of being and working together

One of the most common approaches to workplace culture is also one of the riskiest: assuming adults will simply get it right without guidance.

Sometimes we get lucky, and shared values, goodwill and informal norms are enough to hold a team together for a while. But when culture is left to chance, it often unravels under pressure. Conflict emerges, expectations clash, and leaders are left responding reactively rather than working preventatively.

Research consistently shows that clarity, predictability and shared norms are foundational to psychological safety and effective team functioning (Edmondson, 1999). This is true for adults just as much as it is for children.

All groups benefit from time spent explicitly co-creating how they want to work together. A great starting point is to establish agreed ways of being and working together. Some helpful ways to do this include:

- Hold a brainstorming session that captures what we need from ourselves, our colleagues and our leaders to have a safe and supportive work environment.
- Use workplace values as a guide to these discussions.
- Include examples of what it will look like and feel like when we are operating in safe and supportive ways.
- Plan for how repair will happen. Ruptures are an inevitable part of relationships (including workplace relationships).
- Revisit often.

Building competence

A strong sense of competence is one of the most underestimated contributors to felt safety at work.

Early in my career, I often felt anxious when students became dysregulated, mostly because I didn't know why it was happening or what to do about it. But with appropriate professional learning, support from mentors and opportunities to develop my skills, my confidence grew. In turn my felt sense of safety (and capacity to keep my students safe) grew.

This aligns with research showing that self-efficacy and perceived competence buffer against stress and burnout, particularly in high-emotional-labour roles (Bandura, 1997; Maslach & Leiter, 2016).

Building competence requires more than one-off training. It involves:

- ongoing professional learning that is relevant to the work
- opportunities to practise skills and reflect on real scenarios
- access to mentoring, coaching or peer learning.

If professional development budgets are tight, following mentors online, reading incredible books and identifying colleagues we'd like to learn from are great ways to start sharpening our skills.

Regulation strategies

When people are under sustained stress, the nervous system prioritises survival over reflection, learning and connection. This is well established in neuroscience literature (Porges, 2007; van der Kolk, 2014).

Teams that build shared, accessible regulation practices are better able to stay grounded and think clearly when pressure rises. These practices might include:

- agreed pause points in the day or week
- sensory or grounding resources in shared spaces
- brief check-ins after challenging interactions
- normalising stepping away to regulate, without judgement.

Collective regulation practices support individual regulation. We'll explore this in more depth in chapter 6.

Role clarity

Role clarity means understanding the boundaries, responsibilities and expectations of our work, and having a shared understanding across the team. When roles blur or expand without discussion, people often feel overwhelmed or unsafe.

Research links role ambiguity to increased stress, burnout and reduced job satisfaction (Kahn et al., 1964; Maslach & Leiter, 2016).

This means having shared understanding across the team, and revisiting expectations when roles evolve or change. The task on boundaries we covered in chapter 3 will be really useful here.

Service clarity

Something that helps team members, young people and the broader community to feel safe is knowing exactly what to expect from a service.

Sometimes, I see well-meaning leaders and practitioners stepping outside their scope to support children and families because they feel called to do so. For example, I've seen schools sending teachers to support students at doctor's appointments, and I've seen welfare agencies assign case managers to provide 1:1 reading tutoring to young people.

But when this blurred service happens:

- We create uncertainty and inconsistency for the people we wish to support.
- Our core work may suffer while our time and resources are spent elsewhere.
- Our team members' wellbeing can decline while they juggle competing priorities.

As a team, we can spend some time developing clarity on each role within our school or organisation, before defining what we collectively offer. Then we can be consistent in how we deliver this service, and communicate it clearly with children, young people and the broader community.

Clear processes for supporting challenging behaviours

There is nothing worse than facing a critical incident without knowing what to do or what the workplace protocols look like. This makes an already stressful situation all the more overwhelming.

We can set ourselves up for success by having clear processes in place *and* practising them, through role-plays, scenario planning and reflective discussion, rather than waiting for a critical incident to occur.

Predictable, practised responses reduce cognitive load in high-stress moments and support safer decision-making (Sarmiento et al., 2024). This includes trauma-informed behaviour responses that prioritise safety for everyone involved.

Support with child safety and mandatory reporting

Child safety processes are essential, but fear-based cultures undermine their effectiveness.

When staff are anxious about getting it wrong, they are more likely to hesitate, avoid or make mistakes. I have seen workplaces where staff members are terrified to make a mistake in the reporting processes, with threats of reportable misconduct hanging over their heads and stories of team members who have been investigated.

Of course, these processes are there to keep children safe. But when workplaces are set up in ways that leave people feeling fearful or threatened, we are sending them right back into a survival state where they are much more likely to make a mistake.

If we want child safety to be our core business, we must ensure everyone is confident about their obligations and supported in navigating the processes. This includes space to talk through the emotional toll of these responsibilities, not just the procedural steps.

Regular debriefing or supervision

Debriefing and reflective supervision are consistently identified as protective factors against secondary traumatic stress and burnout (Bride at al., 2007; Fraser & Molineux, 2025).

When embedded into regular practice rather than reserved for crises, supervision supports:

- emotional processing
- skill development
- retention and sustainability.

Clear support pathways

Knowing where to turn when things feel overwhelming reduces isolation and increases help-seeking.

Clear, visible pathways to leadership support, wellbeing roles, peer systems and external services strengthen safety and reduce stigma. Be proactive in accessing these supports and encouraging your team members to access them.

Principle 2: Trustworthiness and transparency

What is it?

Trust is built over long-term consistency. Transparency is a tool that guides the process. When I am talking to groups about trust and transparency, here is what I share:

Staff, children, young people and community members know what to expect and feel informed, included and respected. Trust is built through consistent actions, clear communication, transparent decision-making and professional boundaries.

Why is it important?

Trauma, particularly relational trauma, fundamentally disrupts our capacity to trust. Experiences of abuse, neglect, betrayal or systemic harm shape how people interpret authority, power and intent. When people have been hurt by those who were meant to care for them, their nervous systems adapt to prioritise protection over openness. This shows up in very real ways in our schools and organisations.

Sometimes, our gut instinct tells us not to trust a person or a situation. You know that feeling when something immediately feels a bit off? Often, that instinct is accurate. It's a protective response, informed by past experience.

For others, particularly those who have experienced repeated relational harm, that protective system can remain permanently switched on. Neutral decisions can feel threatening. Lack of information can quickly turn into stories of worst-case intent. Inconsistent communication can be experienced as risk, rather than inconvenience.

From a trauma-informed perspective, this isn't resistance or defiance. It's a nervous system doing its best to stay safe.

To truly establish a trauma-informed culture, we need to ensure that we are showing up consistently, steadily offering transparency and allowing for trust to slowly build.

How do we embed the principle of trustworthiness and transparency?

Trustworthiness isn't built in a single conversation or by one good decision; it's built over time through how we communicate, show up for each other and follow through on what we say we'll do. It depends on how we communicate, how predictable we are, how we handle uncertainty and whether our actions consistently align with our words.

Transparency supports this process: being clear where possible, explaining the reasoning behind changes, and ensuring people aren't left guessing or filling in the blanks with assumptions.

In trauma-affected environments, uncertainty is rarely neutral. Research shows that unpredictability and unclear communication can activate stress responses, particularly for people with histories of relational or systemic harm (Herman, 2015; Porges, 2007).

Predictability, clarity and follow-through help nervous systems settle. When trustworthiness becomes a shared commitment, cultures begin to shift.

Let's look at some strategies to build trustworthiness in our teams and workplace culture.

Communicate openly, honestly and clearly

Open communication doesn't mean sharing everything, but it does mean sharing what we can, when we can. Being honest about what we know and what we don't prevents people from filling in the gaps with worst-case scenarios. Research consistently shows that uncertainty increases stress and threat perception, particularly in trauma-impacted contexts, while clear and timely communication supports psychological safety and trust.

I faced many situations as a school leader where colleagues and young people would look to me for answers that I did not yet have. I'd openly share that reality. I would explain what I knew, what I didn't yet know and what the next steps were. I would also acknowledge that sitting with uncertainty was hard for all of us.

Avoiding jargon, explaining decisions in plain language and checking for understanding all help create shared meaning and reduce misinterpretation.

Follow through on commitments

Trust is built when our actions match our words. If we say we will check in with a colleague, respond to an email or follow up after a meeting, it matters that we do so, and that we do it within the timeframe we've agreed.

Following through demonstrates reliability, which is particularly important in trauma-informed environments where unpredictability has been a common part of the story.

Model and respect clear boundaries

Boundaries provide clarity about what is and isn't okay in our work with colleagues, children, young people and families. When we model them, we show that boundaries aren't about being rigid or unhelpful, they are about creating predictability and safety.

This includes being clear about role responsibilities, availability, decision-making authority and limits. It also includes respecting others' boundaries.

Modelling boundaries also gives others permission to do the same. Research highlights that clear and consistently held boundaries support both trust and psychological safety in teams (Brown, 2018; Edmondson & Harvey, 2018).

Make the 'why' behind decisions visible

People feel more included and respected when they understand the reason behind a decision, especially if that decision impacts their work.

Making the 'why' visible can mean sharing the bigger picture from leadership, linking daily actions to our organisation's vision or mission or explaining why certain processes exist. This helps colleagues, children and families to see the intent behind actions, reducing the chance for assumptions and mistrust.

Own mistakes and share lessons learned

Mistakes are inevitable in complex, human-centred work. What matters most is how we respond when they happen.

Owning mistakes openly and framing them as opportunities for learning sets the tone for a culture of accountability and trust.

When professionals model this behaviour, other members of our communities, including young people, are more likely to admit when they need help, repair relationships faster, and avoid similar issues in the future.

Be consistent in decisions and actions

When we navigate challenges with consistency we build trust. We remove the uncertainty that comes with wondering how a situation will be handled.

Whether it's following the same process after an incident, applying policies fairly or using the same communication channels, consistency shows that everyone is held to the same standard.

When we feel uncertain, our stress response is more likely to be activated, whereas when the environment feels predictable, we can build that felt sense of safety.

Navigate difficult conversations

Instead of allowing frustrations or misunderstandings to grow in the background, develop a workplace culture where colleagues approach each other directly and respectfully to address issues. This fosters respect, prevents gossip and allows problems to be addressed before they escalate.

These conversations are difficult because they often make us feel nervous, uncomfortable or confrontational. It's important to approach these conversations with curiosity, in a regulated state, and with the aim to find solutions together.

You've likely noticed these trauma-informed principles of safety and trust complement each other nicely. The more trust and transparency we have in our team, the safer we are likely to feel. The more safety we have established together, the easier it is to be transparent and work on trusting relationships.

Principle 3: Peer support

What is it?

SAMHSA (2014) defines peer support as:

> A key vehicle for establishing safety and hope, building trust, enhancing collaboration, and utilising stories and lived experience to promote recovery and healing.

When I talk with organisations about peer support, I describe it this way:

> Team members, children, young people and community members benefit from meaningful connections with others who share lived experience or mutual understanding. Peer relationships foster belonging, reduce isolation and create space for healing through shared insight and emotional support. These relationships are facilitated and valued.

Why is it important?

Peter Levine (2010) says, 'Trauma is not what happens to us, but what we hold inside in the absence of an empathetic witness.'

Trauma is profoundly isolating. Often, what makes an experience traumatic is not only what happened, but what we hold inside ourselves (whether that's consciously or unconsciously). We can internalise some difficult messages about ourselves, our experiences and our self-worth.

In 2025 I had the opportunity to speak with a domestic violence survivor on my podcast. He had experienced domestic violence as a child, and then lost his mother to domestic homicide when he was just 15 years old. He shared that he did not meet another domestic homicide survivor until he was in his late 30s, during university study. Hearing others speak about experiences similar to his brought a sense of relief and validation he had not known before. He told me he wished those connections had been available much earlier.

Peer support is increasingly acknowledged in trauma recovery research, highlighting that it provides hope and guidance for the future, improves self-efficacy and lowers stress levels (Wasilewski et al., 2023).

Peer support is also recognised as a wellbeing support for professionals working alongside those who have experienced trauma. A study of child protection workers found peer support to be one of the most utilised and valued wellbeing strategies, often preferred over leadership or external supports. Workers highlighted shared understanding, informal connection, feeling genuinely heard, and humour as key protective factors (Caringi et al., 2016).

I've seen this echoed repeatedly in my own work. Not too long ago, I had the opportunity to work with a team in an alternative school setting to support their staff wellbeing. This setting had particularly high absenteeism, with staff reporting they needed to take days off to support their mental health. When we explored what helped staff continue to show up during difficult periods, one factor stood out above all others: colleague support. They explained it was the informal nature of these relationships, the shared understanding of their experiences and the opportunity to laugh together that aided their wellbeing.

This is just one case study, but it had me reflecting on my own years working as a teacher with trauma-affected young people. In the early days, I'd come home from a stressful experience and offload on my boyfriend or housemates. While they were incredible listeners, they just couldn't quite understand the context of my school. Often, their shock or distress actually amplified my own.

Over time, as I formed deeper connections with colleagues, I found myself leaning less on those after-hours conversations. I had peers who *got it*. People who could hold both the gravity and the absurdity of the work.

Sometimes we find these peers within our schools or organisations, but often we have to look further. Increasingly, I see professionals forming communities of practice, peer networks and reflective groups that offer shared language, shared care and shared responsibility.

No matter where we find these peers, what we are starting to understand is that we all benefit when our experiences are validated and shared with people who understand. It's about knowing we're not alone in the work, that we have colleagues who get it, and that we can share both the challenges and the wins. Building peer support means creating spaces where everyone feels comfortable reaching out, and where that support is met with genuine care.

Peer support is the heartbeat of a trauma-informed team. Here are some actionable steps that can ensure peer support is accessible and celebrated.

Integrating informal peer support

Small, intentional practices can build connection over time. For example, starting team meetings with a brief check-in round allows everyone to share how they are arriving in the day. This not only helps us gauge each other's capacity but also signals that our wellbeing matters. It's important that honest check-ins are modelled and encouraged by members of the leadership team.

Informal peer support is often most impactful when it is consistent, genuine and embedded into the rhythm of our work rather than being a one-off initiative.

Mentoring and being mentored

Whether formal or informal, mentoring relationships can provide a safe space for reflection, guidance and skill growth.

Finding a mentor who understands the unique pressures of our role can be grounding and affirming, while offering mentorship to someone else can strengthen our own practice and sense of purpose. Both roles foster trust and a shared investment in each other's success.

Walk-and-talk practices

Stepping outside the office to discuss challenges or share ideas can make conversations feel more open and less formal. From a trauma-informed perspective, side-by-side conversations minimise stress, and incorporating time in nature can do the same.

Walk-and-talk practices often encourage a different kind of listening and connection. They can be particularly helpful for building stronger relationships, debriefing after intense moments or brainstorming creative solutions.

Between 2021 and 2024, I co-facilitated a wellbeing community for teachers: Teachers' Well. With my Teachers' Well colleagues, Jack Greig and Paul Tupou-vea, we co-designed a simple walk-and-talk structure to support reflective peer connection:

- Walk together side-by-side.
- One person speaks, using the prompts below.
- The listener's role is not to fix or advise, but to keep time and offer reflections such as: 'What I noticed about you …' or 'Based on what you shared, I'm now wondering …'

The prompts:

- Why were you called to this career?
- What values or perspectives feature strongly in your career?
- What is a challenge you are facing in your work?
- Imagine you could look down at your whole career from the top of a mountain. What do you see? What has changed or evolved?
- What is going well?

This kind of structured yet gentle peer reflection supports meaning-making, reconnects practitioners to purpose and strengthens relational bonds, all of which are protective against burnout and secondary traumatic stress (Maslach & Leiter, 2016).

Community circle practices

Circles have been used across cultures for thousands of years as a way of bringing people together in shared humanity. When we sit in a circle, there is no head of the table. Everyone is visible, everyone has equal access to the space, and everyone has the opportunity to speak and be heard.

They can be used for celebration, problem-solving, planning, or debriefing after challenges. Over time, circles build trust, strengthen relationships and create a shared sense of belonging that extends beyond the meeting itself.

Research on restorative and circle-based practices highlights their capacity to build trust, strengthen relationships and improve collective responsibility within groups (Morrison & Vaandering, 2012; Costello et al., 2010). Over time, circles create a shared rhythm of connection that supports belonging and reduces isolation, particularly in high-stress environments.

Embedding reflective practices

Making space for shared reflection, whether in team meetings or smaller peer groups, helps us process our experiences and learn from one another. These moments normalise talking about what's working, what's challenging and how we can support each other moving forward.

Reflection done collectively also strengthens our shared language and approach.

Chapter summary

- Trauma-informed practice is not a quick fix or a single training; it's a way of *being* in our work, woven into everyday relationships, systems and culture.
- The core principles offer a consistent lens for reflection and action at both personal and organisational levels.
- Safety is layered and must be actively restored when lost. It is everyone's responsibility and is co-created through agreements, clarity, competence and shared regulation practices.
- Trustworthiness and transparency grow over time through consistent actions, clear boundaries, honest communication and visible reasoning behind decisions.
- Predictability and follow-through build a sense of stability for staff, young people and communities.
- Peer support is a protective factor for wellbeing in complex work. Informal and formal peer connections reduce isolation, provide validation, foster belonging and create space for shared humour.
- Embedding these principles means working from a place of compassion in action, where safety, trust and connection are lived values, not just stated intentions.

From insight to impact

- **Notice where safety lives.** In your setting, where does safety feel strong and dependable, and where might it be fragile or conditional? What stories do young people and colleagues tell, directly or indirectly, that give you clues?
- **Trace the trust lines.** Reflect on who you trust in your workplace, and why. How might those same conditions be intentionally created for others? Where could greater transparency strengthen relationships or decision-making?
- **Value the everyday peer moments.** Think about the informal connections that make your work lighter or more grounded. How can you protect and grow these moments, even in busy or high-pressure periods?

5

Sharing Power: Collaboration, Choice and Cultural Humility

In earlier chapters, we explored how safety and trust lay the groundwork for trauma-informed practice. Without them, meaningful connection and engagement are difficult to sustain.

This chapter moves us into the next layer of the work: how we share responsibility, honour agency and respond to identity and context within our organisations and communities.

We continue working through the SAMHSA trauma-informed principles, focusing here on collaboration and mutuality; empowerment, voice and choice; and cultural, historical and gender humility and responsiveness. While each principle has its own focus, they are deeply interconnected. Together, they ask us to consider how decisions are made, whose knowledge is valued, how agency is restored, and how identity and history shape people's experiences of safety and belonging.

Trauma-informed wellbeing is not only about reducing harm. It is about creating environments where people can participate meaningfully, contribute from their strengths, and feel seen within the fullness of their cultural and social identities. This requires thoughtful attention to how power operates, but also to how voice is nurtured, how choice is protected and how cultural wisdom is respected.

In this chapter, we explore what these principles look like in practice and how they can be embedded into the everyday rhythms, systems and culture of our workplaces.

Principle 4: Collaboration and mutuality

What is it?

SAMHSA's Trauma and Justice Strategic Initiative (2014) defines the principle of collaboration and mutuality as follows:

> Importance is placed on partnering and the levelling of power differences between staff and clients and among staff, demonstrating that healing happens in relationships and in the meaningful sharing of power and decision-making.

When I talk about collaboration and mutuality in my work with professionals, leaders and organisations, I share:

> Collaboration and mutuality in trauma-informed practice means working together, with everyone's voice and experience valued in decision-making processes. We challenge traditional hierarchies to nurture creativity and trust. We do things with, not to, others.

Why is it important?

Trauma is deeply connected to experiences of powerlessness. Whether through abuse, neglect, coercion, exclusion or systemic harm, trauma often involves having choices taken away, voices silenced or decisions imposed without consent (Herman, 2015).

Due to the loss of control that happens when we experience trauma, we may find ourselves desperate to reclaim that control in order to keep ourselves safe. This is where we really start to grasp the concept of working alongside people, partnering with them and removing power imbalances. When we approach our roles this way, we don't just strengthen relationships; we create the conditions for more creativity, professional and personal autonomy and sustainable solutions.

When we are thinking about collaboration, we are taking care that people are invited in early, not just consulted as an afterthought. We ensure that ideas are genuinely considered and that contributions lead to action, not tokenism.

When we are thinking about mutuality, we are taking care that relationships go both ways. We give and receive feedback, share resources and recognition, and make room for initiative at all levels.

Collaboration and mutuality are everyone's responsibility; they cannot be achieved by leadership alone or left to emerge organically. They need to be embedded into everyday rhythms, systems and culture.

Let's explore how we can build collaboration and mutuality in our teams and workplace culture.

Building structures for shared decision-making

One of the most important shifts we can make is moving beyond consultation towards shared decision-making. This might include rotating facilitation in meetings, setting clear processes for how input is gathered and acted on, and making decision outcomes visible so people can see how their contributions influenced the result.

Co-creating policies and processes

Policies and procedures are often where power is most strongly felt. They shape daily experiences, yet they are frequently written without the voices of those most impacted.

Trauma-informed collaboration asks us to do this differently.

For leaders: when policies, programs or processes are being developed or reviewed, involve staff early, not just at the point of implementation. Working groups, workshops and surveys are not just data-gathering tools, they are trust-building mechanisms.

For team members: asking to be involved, offering ideas or naming what isn't working is not being difficult. It is contributing to a healthier system.

Trauma-informed leaders welcome this input, even when it challenges existing ways of working.

Offering and receiving feedback with curiosity

Feedback can be a mutual exchange, not just a top-down directive. No matter our role, we can start actively seeking feedback from others and offering to provide feedback, too, modelling feedback as a mutual exchange. This normalises learning from each other and strengthens trust over time. Some of the best leaders I have worked alongside have established a culture where they regularly seek feedback from the team to improve their leadership and then generously provide feedback to support individuals to improve their practice.

Sharing resources, recognition and credit

Mutuality is reinforced when we share what helps us do our work well. This might include exchanging tools, templates, strategies or ideas, rather than guarding them as individual expertise. It also means naming contributions out loud and giving credit where it is due, particularly for relational or emotional labour that often goes unseen.

Gather input in varied and equitable ways

Not everyone feels comfortable contributing in the same way, and dominant voices can unintentionally set the tone. Use multiple methods to gather ideas, such as written prompts, one-on-one conversations, small-group discussions, polls, anonymous surveys or structured go-rounds, so all perspectives have space to be heard.

In meetings, note any patterns you notice (for example, the same few people speaking first) and intentionally create opportunities for quieter voices to contribute. These small shifts can elevate the quality and inclusivity of collective decisions.

Principle 5: Empowerment, voice and choice

What is it?

When I talk about empowerment, voice and choice in organisations, this is the end goal I hold:

> Team members, children, young people and community members are recognised as experts in their own lives, with the right to be heard, involved and supported to make meaningful choices. The systems, culture and day-to-day practices around them encourage autonomy, build confidence and enhance strengths, rather than focusing on deficits or compliance.

This principle asks us to move away from doing things *to* people, and towards doing things *with* them.

Why is it important?

Trauma often strips people of agency. Whether through abuse, neglect, coercion, exclusion or rigid systems, traumatic experiences commonly involve a loss of control, voice and choice. Over time, this can shape how people see themselves. They may internalise narratives of helplessness, shame or inadequacy, and begin to doubt their capacity to influence what happens around them (Herman, 2015; van der Kolk, 2014).

Empowerment, voice and choice directly counter these impacts in the following ways:

- Empowerment creates opportunities for people to use their strengths, take initiative and experience themselves as capable and influential.
- Voice ensures perspectives are not only invited, but genuinely heard, respected and acted upon.
- Choice restores autonomy by offering real options in how people work, learn and engage, rather than forcing compliance with a single 'right' way.

When we embed the principle of empowerment, voice and choice, we are supporting the crafting of a more positive narrative about ourselves and others – one that is focused on strengths, self-determination and possibility.

When we bring this principle into our workplaces, we build a healthier culture, where each individual is a valued member of the community, contributing and leading from strength. This helps us craft a positive collective narrative.

So, how can we build empowerment, voice and choice in our teams and workplace culture? Before diving into strategies, it can be helpful to pause and reflect:

- Where do people in our setting have genuine choice?
- Where is voice invited but not meaningfully acted upon?
- How do our systems and habits strengthen people's confidence to contribute?

From there, we can begin to shift practice in practical, achievable ways.

Strengths-based approach

Empowerment grows when we actively challenge deficit-based narratives, both the ones people carry about themselves and the ones organisations sometimes hold about their teams.

Strengths-based approaches invite us to notice what is working, what people bring and how those strengths can be intentionally used. This might look like regularly naming strengths in meetings, feedback conversations or peer acknowledgements. It might also involve reflecting on what your team offers as a collective, and sharing the impact of that work openly.

Research shows that strengths-based practices are associated with higher engagement, increased confidence and lower burnout (Govindji & Linley, 2007; Niemiec, 2018). When people are seen through a strengths lens, they are more likely to step forward and use those strengths.

Choice in how to engage, not just whether to engage

Instead of an 'in or out' approach, offer multiple pathways for engagement. For staff, this might include opportunities to contribute through written reflections, digital tools, small-group conversations, one-on-one discussions or creative expression, alongside traditional meetings.

As leaders, we might offer asynchronous input options (written responses, digital tools) alongside in-person discussions. It might mean giving people a menu of ways to share their perspective – through art, writing, speaking or one-on-one chats. This recognises different comfort levels, communication styles and accessibility needs.

Invite team members to challenge decisions

Trauma-impacted environments can normalise compliance over voice. Actively notice when people are defaulting to 'going along' to avoid conflict or because they believe their view won't matter.

Empowerment requires us to actively notice this pattern and interrupt it.

Creating space for respectful challenge, alternative perspectives and 'yes, and ...' thinking sends a powerful message: your voice matters, even when it differs.

Empowerment, voice and choice thrive when we actively remove barriers, share power and trust people to contribute meaningfully. It's about creating an environment where everyone feels they can say, 'I have something to offer here, and it matters.'

Principle 6: Cultural, historical and gender humility and responsiveness

What is it?

SAMHSA (2014) defines cultural, historical and gender issues as follows:

> The organisation actively moves past cultural stereotypes and biases, offers culturally responsive services, leverages the healing value of cultural connections, and recognises and addresses historical trauma. The organisation incorporates policies, protocols, and processes that are responsive to the racial, ethnic, and cultural needs of individuals served.

The end goal I hold for cultural humility and responsiveness in our organisations is as follows:

> Our teams, children, young people and communities feel their identities, histories and cultures are respected and understood. The systems and everyday practices around them not only avoid harm,

but actively draw on cultural knowledge, connection and wisdom as a source of strength and healing.

Why is it important?

It is impossible to be trauma-informed without acknowledging the deep and ongoing harm that has occurred due to societal structure, systems, policies and practices in our communities. Trauma does not exist in a vacuum. It is shaped by histories of colonisation, racism, gender-based violence, displacement, exclusion and systemic inequity. For many communities, trauma is not only personal or intergenerational, but collective and ongoing.

Once we acknowledge this harm and these injustices, we can work towards equity and justice.

Unlike cultural 'competence', which implies an endpoint or mastery, cultural humility recognises that we never fully arrive. Instead, it asks for lifelong self-reflection, curiosity and a willingness to learn, unlearn and be corrected (Tervalon & Murray-García, 1998).

Responsiveness complements humility by reminding us that cultural safety is not static. It is created and re-created through relationships. What feels safe, respectful or empowering for one person or community may not for another, and those needs can shift over time and context.

Trauma-informed practice that ignores culture, history and gender risks replicating the very harms it seeks to prevent. When we attend to these dimensions thoughtfully, we move closer to equity, trust and genuine healing.

Let's take a look at how we can enhance cultural, historical and gender humility and responsiveness in our teams and workplace culture.

Start with our own cultural stories

Before we can meaningfully engage with others' cultural identities, we need to examine our own. Each of us carries cultural, historical and social influences that shape how we see the world, how we interpret behaviour and how we hold power. Martin Brokenleg (1998) wrote, 'Each of us drags around a cultural tail a thousand years long, as well as our more personal family tale.' This tail (or tale) is a thread of identity, ancestry and experience we carry with us into every space.

Creating time and space for reflection, individually and collectively, helps normalise cultural awareness as an ongoing practice. This might happen through supervision, team conversations or reflective prompts that invite people to explore how their background, values and experiences shape their work, always with choice about what is shared.

Embedding cultural knowledge in everyday practice

Cultural humility moves beyond awareness into action. For those of us working in Australia, this includes recognising that we live and work on the lands of the oldest continuing cultures on earth. Honouring Aboriginal and Torres Strait Islander knowledge, leadership and self-determination is foundational to trauma-informed work in this context.

This means inviting cultural knowledge-holders, Elders or community leaders into the design of programs, policies and practices from the beginning. It might involve integrating language, storytelling, ceremony or community-defined ways of working into the rhythm of the organisation.

Responsive service design

We must adapt the way services are delivered based on cultural and gender needs, such as location, timing, modes of communication, or inclusion of family and community in decision-making.

Flexibility creates respect for the diverse ways people engage.

Self-reflection and bias awareness

Cultural humility requires us to look inwards as much as outwards. This means regularly reflecting on our assumptions, biases and blind spots, especially those shaped by privilege or dominant cultural norms. Structured reflection in supervision, peer conversations or learning led by people with lived experience can support this process.

Attending to gender-based harm and inclusion

Trauma-informed practice must recognise that gender-based violence and discrimination are significant sources of trauma. Ignoring these realities risks reinforcing silence or shame. Responsiveness requires us to build environments where gender diversity is respected and safety is actively protected.

In practice, this might include using inclusive language that does not assume gender identity or family roles, ensuring policies support people across different gender experiences, and creating clear, psychologically safe pathways for reporting harassment or discrimination. It may also involve reflecting on how gender norms shape expectations around leadership, emotional expression, caregiving or authority within teams.

Acknowledging and responding to historical trauma

Recognise the impact of colonisation, displacement and systemic discrimination on the communities we serve. This means naming it openly, not minimising it, and considering how current policies or practices might inadvertently perpetuate harm.

Celebrating cultural diversity year-round

Cultural responsiveness is not achieved through one-off events or calendar acknowledgements.

While celebrations and recognitions matter, they are most powerful when culture is woven into everyday life. This might include sharing food, music, stories and language, or recognising cultural milestones and contributions in meetings and communications.

When celebration is woven into the fabric of the workplace, it reinforces that culture is valued every day, not just on designated occasions.

Cultural humility and responsiveness thrive when we keep listening, keep learning and remain willing to adapt. It's about recognising that we are not the expert on someone else's identity or story, and making room for those who are.

Chapter summary

- Experiences of trauma take away our agency and sense of control. We may then be seeking ways to restore that sense of control. Trauma-informed practice empowers people to restore a sense of agency.
- Collaboration, empowerment and cultural humility are central to embedding trauma-informed practice across all levels of an organisation.
- Collaboration and mutuality focus on sharing power and responsibility, moving from doing *to* towards doing *with*, and fostering genuine participation and collective ownership.
- Empowerment, voice and choice strengthen individual and collective agency by recognising strengths, offering real opportunities for contribution and building confidence through meaningful involvement.
- Cultural humility and responsiveness remind us that safety and wellbeing are inseparable from identity, history and context. They invite ongoing reflection, curiosity and celebration of cultural wisdom.
- Embedding these principles transforms workplaces into communities of care where power is shared, diversity is honoured, and everyone can contribute, learn, and belong.

From insight to impact

- **Map your power structures.** Identify where decisions are currently made and whose perspectives are missing. Invite those voices in early and visibly act on their input.
- **Share and celebrate strengths.** Create regular opportunities to highlight the diverse skills, experiences, and cultural knowledge within your team or community.
- **Practise feedback both ways.** Model curiosity by seeking feedback on your own actions, and show trust by acting on what you hear.
- **Explore your 1000-year-long cultural tail.** Take some time to learn about your own cultural story. Consider your bloodlines, places, practices, rituals and traditions. Share this with a colleague or friend.

6

Spreading Safety or Chaos? The Science of Regulation

I will never forget my first day in the classroom as a graduate teacher. I was teaching maths – a subject way outside my comfort zone – to a group of 16- and 17-year-olds, all residing in residential care.

I spent hours preparing for that first lesson. I refined my lesson plan, I handmade beautiful resources, and I thought I had nailed the fun and engagement side of things.

As I drove to work that morning, my nervous system was going crazy. I was sweaty, my heart rate was noticeably high, and I remember almost missing the turn-off from the freeway (this was also before I owned a smartphone or a car with GPS).

I was riddled with self-doubt. I spent time in the classroom early that morning, setting the furniture, writing on the whiteboard and placing my resources around the room.

Some of my students arrived early for breakfast, and I floated around, saying hi, but barely absorbing a word they said in return. I was so nervous.

When it was time, we walked into the classroom together, and I launched into my well-scripted lesson plan.

It's safe to say it didn't go well.

There were pens all over the floor, and my writing on the whiteboard was replaced with drawings of penises. And my handmade resources? Ripped in half and placed in the bin. My students certainly had fun testing out the graduate teacher.

So, why did it go so wrong? It sounds like I did what all good teachers would do, right? Well, not quite. The best teachers focus on more than lesson plans and resources.

If I could go back in time and redirect my energy, time and focus, I'd place it all on my nervous system and the nervous systems of my students. I'd have scrapped the plans and spent time connecting.

Would it have kept the pens on the desks, the penises off the whiteboard and my handmade resources intact? Who knows. But it would have helped me focus on the one thing I could actually control: myself.

Whether we realise it or not, we're always bringing our nervous system into the room. If I'm dysregulated, anxious or on edge (even if I'm smiling through it), that energy spreads. I've come to understand this now. But back then, I didn't yet have the language or tools to make sense of it.

Regulation is contagious. We're either spreading a sense of safety, or we're unconsciously adding to the chaos.

I remember years later teaching wellbeing science to some of my VCAL students. I shared some of my wellbeing practices with them and told them I meditated each morning before work. One of my students asked if I did that so I could 'put up with them each day'.

We had a bit of a laugh about it, but then I responded that I meditate so they can put up with me.

Working on our nervous system surely increases our tolerance levels, but I'm sure it also makes us more tolerable to those around us. It helps us to show up and be better teachers, youth workers, carers, parents, partners and friends.

So, if I were mentoring that younger version of myself, the one with the colour-coded resources and the panicked drive to work, I wouldn't start with the lesson plan. I'd start with regulation. With the science of safety. With the simple but powerful idea that *how we are* matters more than *what we do.*

The truth is, safety isn't just built through routines or rules. It's built through presence. Through consistency. Through nervous systems that say, 'I'm here, I've got you, and we're okay.'

And that starts with us.

Self-awareness: practising what we preach

You've probably noticed by now that becoming trauma-informed is inner work. To effectively support self-regulation and co-regulation in others, we first need to understand these processes within ourselves.

As a graduate teacher, I had very little understanding of my own regulation. Honestly, I didn't develop that knowledge until later in my career. I spent those early years learning to suppress my emotional and physiological responses to stress.

But here's what I can promise you: I became a much better teacher as my self-knowledge and regulation practices developed. More importantly, I felt better, too.

There are two key areas we can work on:

- Understanding our stress responses – why they happen, how they feel and how they shape our behaviour.
- Identifying strategies to adapt effectively to our environment and stressors.

This is by no means a plea to suppress how we feel or attempt to bio-hack our way to regulation. It's all about recognising our humanness and offering ourselves and others some compassionate ways to navigate our experiences.

Feeling stressed and feeling safe

As we explored in chapter 2, experiencing stress is a pretty normal part of being human. In this chapter, we're going to get more practical and focus on what we can actually do about it. This isn't about removing stress altogether or pretending it doesn't exist – it's about how we respond to it.

Let's go back to the four Fs we covered in chapter 2: fight, flight, freeze and fawn. Together, we explored what they are, what they might be protecting and the linked behaviours we might see in young people and adults. But this only scratches the surface.

What we know is that these responses happen when we feel unsafe. But what happens when we *do* feel safe? What helps us get there? What are the practices we can use for ourselves? What are the practices we can use together?

By the end of this chapter, you'll have explored your own answers to those questions. But first, let's look at why this matters so much.

Polyvagal theory

Many practitioners draw on what is commonly referred to as polyvagal theory to help explain how our nervous system responds to safety, danger and connection. Introduced by Dr Stephen Porges in the 1990s, this framework offers a way of understanding how physiological states shape emotion, behaviour and relationship.

At its core is the idea that our nervous system is constantly scanning for cues of safety or threat, a process sometimes described as neuroception. When we feel safe, our body supports connection, curiosity and flexibility. When we detect danger, our system shifts into survival responses.

It is important to acknowledge that the core insights of regulation and relational safety are not new. First Nations communities across the world, including here in Australia, have long understood the role of connection to land, culture, community, story and rhythm in regulating the body and restoring balance. While polyvagal theory offers a contemporary neurophysiological lens, many of the practices associated with regulation have existed in Indigenous knowledge systems for generations.

While aspects of the neurophysiology continue to be debated in academic circles, the broader clinical insight remains useful: our physiological state profoundly influences how we think, feel, and relate.

We can broadly understand three adaptive response patterns:

- **Mobilised.** When our sympathetic nervous system detects threat, we prepare for fight or flight. We might feel agitated, anxious, angry or overwhelmed. But mobilisation isn't always about danger. When we're safe, mobilisation also fuels excitement, high energy and play.
- **Immobilised.** When our parasympathetic system senses powerlessness or overwhelm, we may feel numb or disconnected. But when we're safe, immobilisation can feel meditative, peaceful or deeply connected.
- **Relaxed.** When our nervous system feels safe enough to rest, connect and create. This is often referred to as the ventral vagal state, a place of curiosity, openness and connection.

These states aren't fixed or linear; we move fluidly between them throughout the day. For example, I might be both mobilised and relaxed when exercising, or relaxed and gently immobilised when meditating or sharing quiet time with someone I trust.

None of these states are good or bad, they are simply our body's adaptive ways of helping us stay safe, connect and function. But when we experience trauma or prolonged stress, our nervous system can become stuck in survival states, finding it harder to return to a relaxed or safe mode.

Understanding these states gives us a language for noticing what's happening inside us, and compassion for how our body is working to protect us. It also sets the foundation for how we can support ourselves and others to regulate more effectively.

The window of tolerance

If polyvagal theory helps us understand what's happening inside the nervous system, the window of tolerance helps us visualise and work with it in practice.

Coined by Dr Daniel Siegel (2012), the window of tolerance is a simple and powerful analogy for our capacity to manage stress and stay regulated.

Within our window

When we are within our window, our nervous system is regulated. We can think clearly, respond intentionally and stay present with others, even if things are a little stressful.

A helpful analogy is to imagine we have a literal window wide open. We only open our windows to the outside world when we're feeling safe. We're not so worried about what might come through the window.

We're more open to others, we can take on more, and it won't impact our capacity or jeopardise our sense of regulation.

Some examples of wide window of tolerance in practice include:

- A youth worker calmly de-escalates a heated conflict between two young people, staying connected and thinking strategically.
- A teacher notices a distressed student, feels compassion and adjusts their activity without feeling overwhelmed.
- A counsellor hears a heavy disclosure but can remain emotionally present and focused on next steps.

Above our window – hyperarousal

When we exceed our window, our sympathetic nervous system takes over. We might feel anxious, angry, or out of control.

Examples might include:

- A residential carer's heart racing after a violent incident, with an urge to flee.
- A domestic violence worker feeling intense frustration and anger at systemic barriers.
- A teacher's defensiveness rising during a challenging conversation with a parent.

Below our window – hypoarousal

When we drop below our window, our system shuts down. We may feel flat, numb or disconnected.

Examples might include:

- A case worker feels powerless to change a situation and shuts down during a planning meeting, unable to take in the conversation.
- After multiple heavy disclosures, an education support worker feels emotionally flat and struggles to show warmth or empathy.
- A youth worker, exposed to ongoing traumatic stories without support, goes through the motions at work but feels disconnected from purpose and meaning.

Our window changes daily. It's shaped not only by what we do for ourselves, but by our environment, team support, clarity of role and the safety of our workplace systems.

Widening our window

Polyvagal theory and the window of tolerance help us understand how our nervous system works to protect and connect us, but insight alone isn't enough. The real power lies in knowing how to work with these states, not against them.

Some questions to reflect on:

- What helps widen your window?
- What narrows it?
- How does it feel when you're above or below your window?
- What could your workplace do to help keep it wide open?

Your answers will give you practical indicators for where to take action, both in your personal regulation strategies and in advocating for team or workplace changes that benefit everyone.

If we think back to the conversation I had with my students about meditation, we were really talking about me putting a practice in place that helped widen my window. For me, regular exercise, good sleep, social connection, and nourishing food also help.

Self-regulation

Regulation is a huge key to our wellbeing, no matter our age or the work we do. When we understand and respond to our emotional and physical needs, we are self-regulating. It's almost impossible to effectively support trauma-affected individuals if we haven't developed a grasp on our own self-regulation.

There's a common misconception that being regulated means being calm. While calm states are wonderful, regulation is not about achieving permanent calm, it's about being able to adapt to what's happening in the moment without tipping into overwhelm or shutting down.

Siegel (2012) describes self-regulation as the capacity to 'remain in a state of balanced activation' that supports social engagement and thoughtful responses to stress.

Murray et al. (2015) describe it as the process by which we adjust mental and physiological states adaptively to context, weaving emotion, behaviour and cognition into a responsive dance towards wellbeing. As we strengthen our capacity for self-regulation, we create the conditions to feel safer.

I like to think about my regulation strategies in two groups:

- **Responsive strategies** I can use when I'm feeling stressed, outside my window of tolerance.
- **Proactive strategies** I can use regularly to support my ongoing wellbeing, widening my window of tolerance.

Drawing our own window of tolerance

To help you understand what your different states feel like and what regulation strategies work for you, I invite you to complete figure 5. If you are new to practising self-regulation activities, that is okay. Please continue reading to see a list of suggested strategies that you might like to try.

Figure 5: Window of tolerance

Above my window (hyperarousal) feels like:	Responsive regulation strategies
Inside my window feels like:	**Proactive regulation strategies**
Below my window (hypoarousal) feels like:	**Responsive regulation strategies**

Examples of responsive strategies:

- Taking a physiological sigh (two inhales through the nose, followed by one exhale through the mouth)
- Planting your feet on the floor and grounding yourself
- Slowly walking around the room
- Engaging the five senses – notice what you can see, smell, touch, hear and taste
- Colouring in or drawing
- Walking side-by-side with someone
- Emotional Freedom Technique (EFT; tapping)
- Body percussion
- Hitting a boxing bag
- Humming
- Drinking some water

Examples of proactive strategies:

- Physical activity or playing a sport
- Meditation
- Yoga
- Journalling
- Eating healthy food
- Limiting caffeine

- Creating a piece of art
- Time in nature
- Time with animals
- Investing in our relationships
- Playing an instrument or singing
- Dancing
- Walking
- Playing with friends and loved ones (yes, adults really need play, too!)

Rhythm and regulation

During my time working in schools, I was also training in the sport of boxing on the side. I was pretty addicted to it. I would head from work to the boxing gym and engage in one to two hours of training most evenings.

There were days when I arrived at the gym fairly exhausted and stressed, my mind racing through the events of the day. But I'd leave the gym feeling peaceful, present and relaxed (so long as it wasn't a heavy sparring session).

I didn't realise at the time, but boxing was providing me with a Patterned Repetitive Rhythmic Activity (PRRA), which stabilises our stress response. Dr Bruce Perry introduced the concept of PRRAs, sharing that simple activities delivered in a patterned repetitive way help to cue our nervous system into safety. As we know, trauma and stress are stored in the body, so talking only gets us so far. Rhythm works at a body-first level, and we're wired for it.

Firstly, we're rhythmic before we're even born. Our first cues of safety come from our mother's heartbeat while we are in the womb. Human development starts in a sound-and-motion bath: maternal heartbeat, respiration and gait create a continuous patterned input for the foetus.

Then, as newborns, we are soothed with rhythm by our caregivers. We cry, they rock us; we get agitated, they dance and gently bounce around the space holding us close. As toddlers, we may have rocking horses, trampolines and swing sets, all providing a PRRA experience.

Across the lifespan, we use rhythmic practices to support our wellbeing. From yoga and breath-led practices that reduce stress symptoms, to group drumming programs that improve mood and social connection, rhythmic interventions have growing empirical support.

Do you already have some PRRAs in your regulation toolkit? Here are some ideas you may like to try:

- Boxing
- Skipping
- Painting
- Knitting
- Breathwork
- Emotional Freedom Technique (EFT; tapping)
- Running
- Music
- Dancing
- Humming
- Rocking chair
- Yoga

What would you add to the list?

PRRAs don't have to be done in isolation. They can be a great way to regulate ourselves alongside our colleagues or the young people we are supporting. Perhaps try out some body percussion games, breathwork before a morning meeting, or using some music and dance together.

Co-regulating dysregulated people

Co-regulation is a supportive process where a caregiver assists a dysregulated person to soothe and manage distressing emotions and sensations.

I like to think of co-regulation as lending our regulated nervous system to someone whose own nervous system is dysregulated. This can only occur when we are regulated ourselves.

It's not easy when we are faced with dysregulated behaviour. As the co-regulator, we're trying to override our own reactivity so we can support someone else's needs. It takes knowledge, practice and self-awareness.

Let's look at some things that help us co-regulate others.

Respond with curiosity

Tapping into our own curiosity assists us to stay in our relational brain and respond with warmth and a sense of calm.

Consider what may have triggered the dysregulation and what it must be like for this person to feel these big emotions and uncomfortable sensations. It can be helpful to voice our noticing and wonderings; for example: 'I notice that this is really hard for you right now. I am wondering if that is because (fill in the blank).'

Remember you are safe

Someone experiencing dysregulation has perceived a lack of safety and they're entering survival mode. It's likely the threat they perceived is not a threat to us. This is particularly true when we are supporting someone who has experienced complex childhood trauma. Their survival system is in overdrive.

Remind yourself that you are safe, the situation is safe and that this person will benefit from the safety cues you provide.

If the cognitive practice of thought is less available to you at the time (once you're feeling a bit stressed), you can use one of your responsive regulation strategies (e.g. a physiological sigh or planting your feet firmly on the ground) to rebalance your own nervous system before tending to theirs.

Allow yourself to be co-regulated by others

It's okay not to be the master co-regulator all of the time! We're human beings doing some tough work. When needed, give yourself the opportunity to borrow someone else's regulated nervous system for a while. Share the job of co-regulation.

Creating regulating environments

Self-regulation and co-regulation are powerful tools, but they're most effective when the environment around us supports them.

A regulating environment is one that reduces unnecessary stress, increases cues of safety and provides predictable patterns. It's an environment that helps us stay inside our window of tolerance more often, and gives us pathways back when we step outside it.

This isn't about creating a perfect space where nothing ever goes wrong – that's not realistic. It's about making intentional choices in the way we set up our physical spaces, structure our time and interact with one another.

Some key elements of a regulating environment include:

- **Predictability:** Clear routines, visible schedules and consistent processes that we can rely on. Predictability reduces uncertainty, which is why the brain interprets predictability as a safety cue.
- **Sensory awareness:** Attention to noise levels, lighting, temperature and clutter. Too much sensory input can push us above our window; too little can leave us feeling flat or disconnected.
- **Opportunities for movement:** Incorporating physical activity into the day, from formal breaks to micro-movements such as stretching, standing or short walks.
- **Access to regulation tools:** Spaces or resources that we can use when we feel stressed (e.g. quiet rooms, sensory kits, art materials and music).
- **Cues of connection:** Warm greetings, making eye contact when appropriate, using names and showing genuine interest in each other's lives.
- **Shared responsibility for wellbeing:** Everyone in the team contributes to maintaining a safe and supportive environment. It's not the role of one person, it's the collective.

When I think back to the most regulating workplaces I've been part of, they weren't always the calmest or most zen spaces. They were often busy and full of life, but they had an underlying structure and culture that made it safe to show up as we were.

We could be stressed, we could be tired, we could even be in conflict, and there was still a sense that this was a place where we belonged, where we could repair when things went wrong, and where we could get the support we needed to keep going.

Creating a regulating environment is an ongoing process. It evolves with the people in it, the challenges faced and the work being done. But the more intentional we are, the more likely we are to create a space where regulation is possible – for us, for our colleagues and for the young people we support.

Chapter summary

- Regulation is not about always being calm; it's about having the capacity to respond intentionally to what's happening around us.
- Polyvagal theory helps us understand the biological foundation of safety and connection, how our nervous system shifts between states of mobilisation, immobilisation and calm depending on the cues we perceive in our environment.
- Our nervous system states are contagious; we are always influencing those around us, for better or worse.
- The window of tolerance helps us understand when we're regulated, when we're in hyperarousal (above our window) and when we're in hypoarousal (below it).
- Self-regulation strategies can be responsive (used in the moment of stress) or proactive (built into our daily routines to sustain wellbeing).
- Patterned repetitive rhythmic activities (PRRAs) are powerful for stabilising our stress response, as our brains and bodies are wired for rhythm.
- Co-regulation is the process of lending our regulated nervous system to another person who is dysregulated – and we can only do this effectively when we are regulated ourselves.
- Regulating environments reduce unnecessary stress, increase cues of safety and provide predictable patterns that help us stay inside our window of tolerance.

From insight to impact

- **Map your strategies:** List your own responsive and proactive regulation strategies on your window of tolerance. Consider how these support your nervous system state and energy.
- **Build PRRAs into your workday:** Identify at least one rhythmic activity you can incorporate regularly, whether it's a walk, music, tapping or movement before a meeting.
- **Shape your environment:** Choose one change you can make to your workspace, schedule or team routines that will add predictability or reduce unnecessary stress cues for you and your colleagues.

7

Supporting Behaviour Without Sacrificing Wellbeing

Our whole approach to human behaviour is wrong.

Sound bold?

I wish I could write it on each and every page of this book. Because it needs to be said, to everyone, loudly and often, until we start seeing real change.

We start building and weaving some beautiful, human-centred, wellbeing-informed practices into our workplaces – practices grounded in safety, care, connection and predictability.

And then we pull the thread right back out with our punitive behaviour-management approaches.

If we think of our relational culture as a nest, every interaction is part of the weave. Every moment of steadiness strengthens it. Every compassionate response adds another secure strand.

Our punitive responses – shame, blame, exclusion, harshness – act like a hand ripping twigs out from underneath us. The nest becomes less stable, less safe, less able to hold anyone's weight.

As a broader society, we see behaviour through a black-and-white lens. There's good behaviour, which gets rewarded, and bad behaviour, which gets punished. We believe that's enough to motivate people: chase the rewards, avoid the punishments.

But we have decades of evidence showing it doesn't work. We have stressed educators, struggling systems and young people being excluded from the very environments designed to support them.

We have workplaces that are reactive, rather than reflective. And we have professionals questioning why the same cycles keep repeating. More plans, more policies, more exclusions yet no real change.

The truth is, we've misunderstood what behaviour is. We've moralised it, labelled it and divided it into categories that make us feel in control – but behaviour isn't about control. It's communication. It's biology. It's context. It's story.

Some of us even talk about good people and bad people, but where do these so-called bad people come from? Were they just born that way?

Research suggests not. In one American study, adults in prison reported nearly four times as many adverse childhood experiences as the general population (Franco et al., 2013). In Australia, a 2022 study found that 89 per cent of young people in the youth justice system had experienced childhood maltreatment (Cale et al., 2022).

That's not coincidence. It's correlation – a connection between early harm and later behaviour. And yet, as a society, we continue to respond to harm with more harm.

I became a teacher because I wanted to work with young people. I wanted to make a difference. I believe education opens doors to a future. Teachers are there to show young people those doors exist.

But too often, our systems show them a different door – *the exit door.* Out of the classroom, out of the school and out of the community.

From a trauma-informed perspective, exclusionary practices ignore what we know about the human stress response. They reinforce attachment ruptures and compound the shame already carried by young people who've experienced adversity. And, they are a missed opportunity to support someone who needs it most.

I know supporting behaviour can be difficult, exhausting, even scary at times. I know the impact on wellbeing when our classrooms or workplaces feel unpredictable or unsafe.

But I also know we've been misled about behaviour. We've been taught to use frameworks and policies that go against our values, that tell us to punish what we should be understanding, to control what we should be co-regulating and to fix what we should be healing.

It's not working.

It's time to do this differently. Very differently.

Behaviour isn't black and white; it's human. It sits in the grey – in stress responses, unmet needs and moments of overwhelm.

What I want to explore in this chapter is how we can respond to behaviour in ways that feel good for us, that feel good for young people, and that keep the doors to the future wide open.

We're struggling to support young people with behaviour because we've been lied to

Not long ago, I attended an expo for first- and second-year teachers to talk about wellbeing. I asked each of the teachers I met a simple question: 'What are you noticing about your wellbeing?' I kept it deliberately open, to see where they'd take it.

Every single teacher spoke about behaviour. They described behaviour as more severe than expected, more exhausting, more time-consuming. They were overwhelmed and, in their words, 'It's not what we were prepared for.'

It made sense. I'd been delivering a series of workshops on behaviour and hearing the same story everywhere: teachers feeling defeated, questioning themselves and wondering why nothing seemed to work. Most entered the profession as content experts, passionate about their subject area, eager to inspire learning, and were led to believe that success meant a quiet classroom and a well-executed lesson plan.

But what's really at the core of teaching?

Human beings. Young, developing, emotional, social, complex human beings.

We send these children and young people into busy hubs with hundreds, sometimes thousands, of others, full of sensory stimulation, social dynamics and unspoken expectations. Then we ask them to sit still, stay calm, follow instructions perfectly and perform on demand for up to 30 hours a week.

That's a tall order for anyone, let alone someone whose brain is still wiring itself for emotional regulation, relationships and safety.

When we ignore this reality, we ignore their humanness. And we design systems that set both students and teachers up to fail.

If I measured my success as a teacher by how quiet my classroom was, I would have been a failure.

So, this chapter isn't about managing behaviour, it's about understanding it. It's about the behaviour of children and young people, our own behaviour, and the collective behaviour of the systems we work in. It's about redefining success, away from control and compliance, and towards connection, regulation and growth.

The behaviour paradox

I've always been deeply curious about human behaviour. I've spent years working alongside young people who present with a whole spectrum of behaviours, from the gentle and the quirky to the loud, disruptive and complex.

But the further into this work I go, the more I'm struck by something glaring: *our expectations of a young person's behaviour are often wildly unrealistic*, whether they've experienced trauma or not.

The biggest piece of evidence I have for this bold statement? Adults.

These days, most of my work is with adults – educators, mental health professionals, youth workers, foster and kinship carers and parents. Sometimes we're together for an hour, sometimes for several days.

And honestly? Teaching adults isn't that different from teaching young people. We're all human, and our behaviour is always communicating something.

In fact, just last week, I had a few moments in training sessions that could easily have been mistaken for teenage behaviour, but came from grown adults. These adults were across different organisations and from different sectors. The behaviour included:

- **The sword request.** During an activity where participants could anonymously share what they needed from me, from themselves and from each other to create a safe and engaging session (an activity that participants usually take quite seriously), one person wrote: 'a big sword'. I read it back to the group in a lighthearted way, curious about the response. It turned out this joke came from a member of the leadership team, and was an in-house joke that not all participants were privy to.
- **The sensory item collector.** Before a workshop, I placed regulation tools and sensory items on each table. As people arrived, one participant walked around the room inspecting each table's supplies, selected their favourites and returned to their own table with a personalised stash, leaving some of the other tables bare.
- **The technology avoider.** In an online session, one participant had some tech issues. They announced to the group that they felt unsafe because the technology wasn't working, and then didn't engage for the rest of the session.
- **The hysterical laugher.** While co-designing an implementation plan with a group, one participant could not stop laughing and chatting with her peers. She said she hadn't slept well the night before and was having trouble concentrating.

I don't share these examples to embarrass anyone; in fact, quite the opposite. They're reminders that behaviour is simply the outward expression of what's going on internally. It's human. It's not just *kids*. It's not just those who are impacted by trauma who express their needs through behaviour. We all do it.

Of course, I followed up with these people individually, checking how they were tracking and how I could continue to support them. And that's what I would do for young people, too.

If a young person broke out in hysterics during a group activity, or someone refused to verbally contribute, I'd just want to see how I could best support them and offer some alternative options for them to engage.

Some participants don't want to speak during a session, which I completely respect and make space for; however, in many schools, cold calling (picking a student to answer on the spot) is still a common practice. We expect young people to speak up when we demand it, even though many adults would prefer to opt out as well.

If we drop the unrealistic expectation that children and young people should behave better than adults often do, we create space for compassion, curiosity and more effective support.

And we might just feel more competent and less exhausted, too.

Defining behaviour

At its most basic, behaviour is *how someone acts*. But reducing it to just an action misses the richness of what's going on beneath the surface.

For human beings, behaviour was our earliest form of communication. Before we had words, our bodies did the talking. As newborns, we cried when we were hungry or uncomfortable, reached out when we wanted to be held, and screamed or shrieked when we felt unsafe. Our behaviour was the only tool we had to express our needs and connect with the people around us.

That hasn't changed as much as we might think. Whether we're three years old, 13 or 83, our behaviour is still a form of communication. It's meeting a need, expressing a feeling or responding to the environment.

Behaviour always serves a purpose, no matter our age or stage of development. Some of those purposes include:

- **Communication and self-expression.** A young person might slam a door not just to be rude, but because they can't find the words to say, 'I'm hurt and I don't know how to tell you.' An adult might send a blunt email rather than expressing frustration face-to-face.
- **To obtain something.** This could be tangible, such as food, or intangible, such as connection or reassurance. For example, a child may repeatedly ask questions during a lesson to seek proximity to a trusted teacher. An adult might make a joke in a tense meeting to get a laugh and gain acceptance from their colleagues.
- **To avoid something.** This could be avoiding a task, an environment or an emotional risk. A young person might skip class to avoid being humiliated when they don't understand the content. A professional might find reasons to reschedule a difficult conversation with a colleague.
- **To protect ourselves.** When we are feeling stressed or unsafe, our behaviour might solely be about protecting ourselves. A young person might make verbal or physical threats to keep people away. An adult might become defensive and loud when they're emotionally exhausted.

These actions aren't just good or bad, they're adaptive. They've been learned, often over years, to help the person survive or to meet a need. Even behaviours that seem disruptive, defiant or self-sabotaging are usually the most accessible or familiar strategies that a person has in that moment.

Understanding this can help us shift our lens from 'What's wrong with you?' to 'What's happening for you?' We start to see behaviour as data, as part of this person's story, not a problem to be eliminated. This opens the door to curiosity, compassion and more effective responses.

Befriending our own adaptive and protective behaviours first

You guessed it: we're looking towards ourselves again. Because the truth is, we cannot change the behaviours of those around us, but we can work on changing our own. The more we can recognise in ourselves, the better we become at empathising with and supporting others.

Our early life experiences don't just shape our brain development, nervous system and relationships; they also create a template for our behaviours. Sometimes these behaviours are shaped in ways that serve us well. Other times, they are shaped in adaptive ways – strategies we developed to survive and meet our needs in less-than-ideal circumstances.

I have some early memories of going out for a family dinner once a month. My brother and I would be told to dress nicely, be quiet at the dinner table and act like grown-ups. We would politely thank the restaurant staff and be praised by our parents for being such good kids afterwards. Those dinners gave me a template for how to behave in public, how to be polite with strangers, and left me grateful to those who work in hospitality or service – all behaviours I've carried into adulthood.

But I also experienced neglect in my childhood. I spent a lot of time alone as a child. I learned to cook at an unusually young age, spent nights sleeping in a house by myself, solved daily problems most people don't figure out until young adulthood, and got a job before the legal working age.

This neglect gave me a template for how to be fiercely independent, how to not ask others for help or support, and left me believing that I needed to know how to rely on myself, because others won't be reliable.

So, I learned to meet my needs by adapting my behaviour. For a long time, I believed these behaviours meant something was wrong with me. Now, I understand them as reflections of what happened to me (or what didn't happen, in this case).

These adaptive behaviours made me feel safe. They became comfortable. And they worked – they kept me alive.

This template is still familiar to this day. My nervous system and my body relax when I've taken charge, solved something without asking for help and met my own needs. But I know that human relationships thrive when we let people in, when we allow them to help us, and when we let them deeply know us. And professionally? I can't do this work alone. We absolutely can't.

It's a team effort. I don't have all the answers, and hyper-independence is a straight road to poor decisions and burnout.

This has been a big part of my life's work: recognising the early templates for my behaviour, stepping into the uncomfortable and allowing new templates to be written alongside the old ones.

This takes practice, and it takes support. But I'm a fan of getting comfortable with being uncomfortable, because that's where growth happens. I'm deep in this work, knowing it's worth it.

So here's my invitation to you. Take some time to consider your early life experiences and the norms of your childhood household. This can be a powerful journalling exercise. Consider the following questions:

- In childhood, what was I explicitly taught about behaviour?
- What experiences may have created a template for my behaviour?
- How have my behaviours met my needs or supported my survival?
- What opportunities might open if I challenged my adaptive behaviours?
- What do I need to support myself as I challenge these behaviours?

Behaviour management?

One thing I can promise you as a professional working alongside children and young people is that you will be exposed to a wide range of behaviours.

Some will challenge you. Some will cause concern. Some may feel completely out of control. It will happen, often.

But behaviour management isn't really about managing *them*. It's about managing ourselves so we can effectively empower and support young people.

It's about noticing how we are, what we can handle and how we're responding in the moment. It's about recognising when our own nervous system is becoming activated, when frustration, exhaustion or helplessness start creeping in, and choosing to pause, breathe and respond rather than react.

When we take this approach, we shift from controlling behaviour to *modelling regulation*. Every look, tone and gesture becomes a teaching moment. Young people don't just hear what we say; they feel the state we're in and see who we are.

I prided myself on being pretty good at this practice as a teacher. That's why I'll never forget a day when I didn't do it so well. I was tired and frustrated, and I reacted to my class. I lost my patience, I raised my voice and I took them all by surprise. The next day, I took it as a learning opportunity. I apologised to my students and told them exactly what had happened: that I'd reacted instead of responding. We ended up having an impromptu lesson on the difference between the two: reacting from stress versus responding from awareness. They loved it. We laughed, reflected and talked about how we could all practise noticing those moments in ourselves.

That day reminded me that our calm is contagious, but so is our chaos.

Explicitly naming our own emotional states throughout the day – 'I'm starting to feel frustrated, so I'm going to take a breath before we move on' – is one of the most powerful forms of emotional literacy we can teach. It shows young people that emotions aren't dangerous; they're data. It gives them permission to notice, name and regulate their own states, too.

Supporting young people with behaviour and feeling good about it

I need to take a big sigh before writing this section.

Okay. Here goes.

Punitive approaches to behaviour rarely achieve the outcomes we're looking for. In fact, they can erode trust, damage relationships and, if we're honest with ourselves, they feel pretty awful to enforce.

Before going any further, it's important to be clear about what I mean when I use the word 'punishment'. When I'm talking about punishment in this book, I'm referring to approaches that are primarily about control, compliance or payback, rather than learning, repair or restoration. Punishment often carries outdated assumptions, such as:

- isolating a young person from others without supporting repair or reconnection

- removing support until a child has paid for their behaviour
- enforcing consequences with little regard for context, stress or underlying need
- prioritising rule enforcement over relationship, dignity or safety.

I want to name that punishment is not the same thing as boundaries, expectations or natural and logical consequences. We'll unpack this distinction later in the book, because consequences absolutely have a place in safe, trauma-informed environments. But punishment, as defined above, is something different.

If you take some time to read the latest research around moral injury in teachers, what you'll notice is that enforcing punitive behaviour-management strategies is a high risk to our wellbeing. We're asked to prioritise standardised tests, punish children for wearing the wrong shoes and exclude a child who acted out of distress in our classroom, knowing full well they have nowhere to go when they don't come to school.

Now that we have explored so much of what behaviour is and where it comes from, it can seem a little absurd that we want to try to control the behaviour of young people.

That doesn't mean we create spaces with no structure or boundaries. Safe spaces are not unstructured spaces.

It means we move away from crime and punishment thinking and towards approaches that support growth, restore safety and model the kinds of behaviours we actually want to see.

Here are some tips for supporting behaviour that feel good to put into practice, and that actually work to support growth and change.

Prioritise relational safety first

Walking into a new school year or new classroom can send the nervous system spiralling. Young people are socially driven, and one of their biggest concerns is whether they will be accepted and belong in this school or classroom community.

If we want some regulated nervous systems in the room, we need to address this need first and foremost. We can build rapport with each of these young people, we can set the tone of warmth and care, and we can facilitate opportunities for these young people to connect with each other.

Unconditional positive regard

When behaviour challenges us, it's easy to slip into judgement or frustration, but unconditional positive regard reminds us to separate the person from their actions. To hold on to their dignity and worth, even when their behaviour is difficult.

You're not excusing harm; you're recognising their humanity. This stance keeps the relationship intact and models the kind of compassion that makes repair possible.

We'll unpack this concept in depth in chapter 8.

Co-create the norms of the space

When young people are part of setting the expectations, they're more invested in upholding them. Co-creating norms means inviting them into the conversation: 'What makes a space feel safe for you? What helps you feel respected here?'

It shifts the dynamic from rules imposed *on* them to agreements made *with* them. This not only builds ownership but also makes it easier to address behaviour later: you're referring back to a shared agreement, not enforcing a personal power move.

When behaviour challenges these norms, we now have a common language to talk about what happened and how we can restore it.

See behaviour as a skill that can be developed with support

We teach reading. We teach maths. We teach children how to ride a bike. Yet when it comes to behaviour, we often expect young people to just know what to do.

Behaviour can be taught in the same way we teach any skill: with clear modelling, step-by-step scaffolding and chances to practise without fear of punishment.

When something goes wrong, we can bring our curiosity to help us understand the situation. *What skills, resources or support does this child need?*

This might mean role-playing a tricky social situation, using social stories, breaking down the steps of how to regulate after getting frustrated, and practising repair with peers and adults.

When we see behaviour as something that can be learned and strengthened over time, we replace judgement with curiosity.

Lean on natural consequences rather than punitive ones

Natural consequences are outcomes that flow logically from the behaviour itself, without shaming or inflicting unrelated punishment.

Some examples:

- **Damaging furniture or property in anger:** When regulated again, the young person helps repair or repaint the item, connecting their action to restoration and pride in shared spaces.
- **Disrupting learning:** If a student repeatedly interrupts during group time, the natural consequence might be taking a short break to reset, then rejoining when ready, instead of being sent out for the entire session.
- **Ignoring group agreements:** If a student speaks over others in circle, the natural consequence might be losing speaking time that round and reflecting together on how to make the next round feel fair for everyone.

This approach helps young people connect cause and effect, without attaching fear or resentment to the process. It also models fairness and empathy: you're not punishing *them* as a person, you're addressing the *action* and making space for repair.

Use co-regulation as a first response

When a young person is dysregulated, their capacity for reasoning, problem-solving and impulse control is reduced. Meeting them in that moment with calm, regulated presence can make all the difference.

This might look like lowering your voice, slowing your speech, mirroring their breathing or simply sitting nearby until they're ready to talk. Co-regulation isn't about fixing the behaviour instantly; it's about helping their nervous system return to a state where they *can* engage with expectations and problem-solve together.

Ask reflective questions to invite insight

Once emotions have settled, shift from telling to asking. Reflective questions help young people make sense of what happened and consider alternative responses.

Some examples:

- What was going on for you just before that happened?
- What might help you handle it differently next time?
- What do you need from me to make that easier?

This positions them as an active participant in the process, not a passive recipient of discipline, and reinforces that behaviour is something they can shape over time.

Rupture and repair: the golden nugget in transforming behaviour

In trauma-informed work, rupture is inevitable. Whether it's a tense exchange in a meeting, a misunderstanding during a shift change or a heated moment with a young person, moments of disconnection will happen.

What matters most is what we do next. Repair is where trust is rebuilt, safety is reinforced and learning happens for everyone involved.

Restorative practices offer a way forward that move us beyond blame and punishment. Instead, they help us focus on understanding the impact of actions, acknowledging needs and finding a way to move forward together.

With young people, this might look like sitting alongside them after a difficult moment and asking, 'What happened for you there?' With colleagues, it might mean making space to name the tension and explore what each person needs for the relationship to feel safe again.

When I was a school leader, a large part of my work was supporting young people through restorative practices. I remember one young man who enrolled in our school and engaged in a record number of restorative meetings. It felt like I was constantly on my toes, hearing from others that something had gone wrong, spending my day trying to track him down, and working through what had happened. But I also knew nobody in his life had ever supported him in navigating conflict and repair before.

At the time, he was bouncing between staying with different family members and had been rejected from other schools. So, we kept going. We kept meeting. We kept unpacking what had happened, how we could repair, how we could regulate next time and what support he needed.

And then, something amazing happened: I didn't have to chase him anymore.

He started knocking on my office door, telling me he felt dysregulated and asking to punch some pads or go for a walk. He began letting me know when he needed to repair with someone.

Soon after, we were meeting less often; eventually, we didn't need those meetings at all.

Many traditional conflict-resolution approaches assume that people can regulate, take perspective and problem-solve in the moment. But trauma, stress and neurodiversity can make these skills harder to access, especially when emotions are high. That's where Collaborative Problem Solving (CPS), introduced by Ross Greene (2008), offers an alternative.

CPS begins with empathy: truly listening to understand the other person's perspective and unmet needs. It then moves to clearly defining the shared problem and brainstorming solutions that work for both parties.

This process builds trust, models respectful communication and supports skill-building over time. With young people, CPS might mean slowing down to understand what's getting in the way of meeting an expectation. With colleagues, it could mean recognising when workload, unclear processes or relational dynamics are fuelling the tension, and working together to address them.

When we apply rupture-and-repair thinking consistently, across our work with young people and in our teams, we create cultures where relationships are resilient, conflict becomes an opportunity for growth, and trust can withstand the challenges that inevitably arise in complex work.

Holding compassion for adult behaviour

Taking on this work isn't easy. It can be incredible, but it's also demanding, and by now, we know that ongoing stress impacts our body, brain and behaviour.

When we see stress responses in the young people we support, we usually have empathy. But when those same stress responses show up in adults – our colleagues, leaders or even ourselves – our compassion can fade.

Just like young people, adults communicate through behaviour. Irritability, withdrawal, micromanaging, avoidance and sarcasm are often the adult versions of fight, flight, freeze or fawn. They're signals of stress, not character flaws.

When we approach adult behaviour with the same curiosity and care we offer young people, we strengthen trust, reduce conflict and model what trauma-informed culture really looks like. It's not about excusing harm or ignoring accountability; it's about remembering context.

A trauma-informed workplace doesn't expect people to perform perfectly at all times. It acknowledges that we will all have days when we're running on empty, carrying stories we can't name or reacting from our own history.

When we extend unconditional positive regard to the adults around us, we humanise our workplaces and reduce the very stress that fuels the behaviours we find hardest to manage.

Because if behaviour is communication, then every adult is communicating, too.

Chapter summary

- We cannot control others' behaviour, and doing so is not a measure of our competence.
- Behaviour is communication, for young people and adults alike, shaped by needs, experiences and context.
- Punitive measures rarely work and can harm trust, relationships and wellbeing.
- Our spaces need structure, which can be built with respect, shared ownership and skill-building.
- Our own adaptive behaviours deserve reflection. Knowing our early behaviour templates helps us decide what to keep, challenge or change.
- Success is not compliance or silence; it's safety, connection, repair and growth.

From insight to impact

- **Reflect on your own behaviour templates.** Consider the early life experiences and environments that shaped how you respond under stress, set boundaries or handle conflict. Which behaviours have served you well? Which ones might be holding you back in your work or relationships? Make space to practise small changes and notice their impact.
- **Redefine what success looks like in your context.** Move away from measuring effectiveness by compliance, quietness or the absence of conflict. Instead, focus on indicators such as safety, connection, trust and regulation. Share this reframing with your colleagues or team so you can work towards a shared vision of success.
- **Co-create norms and teach behaviour as a skill.** Involve young people in setting the agreements for your space, and treat behaviour as something that can be learned, practised and refined.
- **Practise repairing after a rupture.** Lead with empathy, consider what may have happened for the other person during the rupture, and work together to solve the problems.

Part III

Strengthen

> strengthen *verb*
> to make something stronger or more effective, or to become stronger or more effective.
>
> *Cambridge Dictionary*

We strengthen our practices, relationships and systems so that they can hold steady under pressure. This stage is about building capacity, resilience and alignment, ensuring that the principles of trauma-informed practice are lived out consistently, even when challenges arise. It's where leaders reinforce the conditions that allow their teams and communities to flourish.

8

The Relationship Blueprint: Belonging, Trust and Unconditional Positive Regard

In the NEST framework, belonging and relationships live in the strengthen stage because that's exactly what belonging does: it strengthens us.

Birds don't wait for a storm to arrive before weaving their nests. They build long before the winds pick up. Strand by strand, twig by twig, they create something that can hold weight, weather and friction.

Relationships work the same way. When we invest early and often, we create the weave that holds us, and each other, steady when the challenges hit.

For professionals working in trauma-affected spaces, this weave of belonging is not an added luxury – it is what supports us to stay.

Marcus's story

Name and details changed to protect identity

I've spent much of my career working alongside children and young people who have experienced significant trauma. Many lived in out-of-home care, moved between placements and experienced repeated disruptions to their education, relationships and sense of safety. Over time, I found myself returning to the same question: *What helps some young people move towards positive outcomes, even after everything they have lived through?*

Marcus is one of those young people.

Marcus entered the out-of-home care system early in life and spent much of his childhood moving between placements. By the time he was a teenager, he had experienced school exclusion, involvement with the justice system and long periods of instability. His behaviour made sense when you understood the context, but there were also days when it felt exhausting, demanding and relentless for the adults around him.

What changed Marcus's trajectory was not a single intervention or program. It was the presence of safe adults consistently showing up.

At a critical point in his adolescence, Marcus was enrolled in a school that did not expel him or exclude him when things became difficult. Around the same time, his residential care placement stabilised. Two relationships became anchors in his life: a house manager who treated him with care and consistency, and a teacher who showed up, day after day, even when Marcus tested every boundary.

Over time, the chaos settled. His risk-taking behaviours slowly reduced. He began attending school regularly. He found part-time work. He completed his senior year of school. Slowly, a future that once felt impossible began to feel imaginable.

Marcus is now an adult. He lives independently, works full-time, has interests and hobbies and is exploring further study. When he reflects on what made the difference, he does not talk about programs or specific interventions. He talks about relationships. About knowing he would see the same adults day after day.

And I know this story intimately, because I was one of those adults.

Marcus's outcomes were only possible because the adults around him were supported enough to stay.

They worked within teams that prioritised relationships. They were held by leadership that understood the emotional weight of the work. They had access to training, debriefing and shared responsibility. They were not doing this alone.

This chapter is about how we create the conditions for us, the adults, to belong at work and to feel relationally connected, so we can keep showing up with consistency, care and humanity. Because when we are unsupported, burnt out or isolated, the cost is not only personal; it is carried by the young people who experience yet another adult leaving.

If we want different outcomes for children and young people like Marcus, we must take practitioner wellbeing and belonging seriously.

Relationships predict and protect wellbeing

If you take just one thing from this book, please let it be this: *relationships change lives.*

Relationships are the strongest predictor of our wellbeing and one of the most powerful protective factors we have. You would be hard-pressed to find a credible wellbeing framework that does not place relationships at its core.

In fact, in an 85-year study of human happiness, now known as the Harvard Study of Adult Development, Waldinger (2023) found that strong relationships were associated with better health, greater wellbeing and longer lives. Beginning in 1938, the study followed two very different groups of young men in Boston: 19-year-old Harvard students and a cohort from disadvantaged neighbourhoods. Over time, these studies merged into one cohort of 725 men, and later expanded to include their partners and children.

The findings were clear. It was not wealth, status or achievement that predicted who stayed healthiest. It was the quality and warmth of their relationships. People who felt more connected to others lived longer and experienced better physical and mental health.

Researchers suggest that close relationships act as stress regulators. They help our bodies settle and return to equilibrium after stress, lowering the risk of chronic illness, cognitive decline and long-term health issues.

This makes sense. As we explored earlier in this book, we are relational beings. From infancy, we rely on caregivers to help regulate our stress. As we grow, peers, partners and colleagues take on this role. We are not designed to simply manage stress alone.

When trauma occurs early in life, this process of relying on others is disrupted. Relational templates are shaped by unpredictability, threat or harm. Closeness can feel unsafe. Trust can feel risky. This is especially true for the trauma-impacted young people we walk alongside. They may want connection deeply, while also resisting it. This is not a deficit. It is a survival response.

And many of you reading this are the consistent adults in their lives.

If you are a full-time teacher, for example, you spend around 180 days each year with your students. That is 180 opportunities for connection; 180 chances to show consistency, predictability and care; 180 moments to prove that others can be reliable.

I know I'm preaching to the converted. You chose this work because relationships matter to you. You already understand the power of showing up, of consistency, of being someone young people can rely on.

What we are often less explicit about is what we need in order to keep doing this work.

If relationships are central to wellbeing, then they matter just as much for us as they do for the people we support. That includes knowing we are held by others, and that we have places to offload, to be understood, to regulate and to reconnect.

Relational work asks something of us every day. It draws on our patience, our empathy and our energy. I often remind professionals that we're not in a two-way compassionate relationship with the children and young people we care for; we give out much more compassion than we receive in return, so we need to be mindful of the relationships that can sustain us, too, and how we can offer relational safety to our teams and colleagues.

Belonging in our work communities strengthens us, too. And it is one of the reasons people choose to stay.

The pain of not belonging

> A deep sense of love and belonging is an irreducible need of all people. We are biologically, cognitively, physically and spiritually wired to love, to be loved, and to belong. When those needs are not met, we don't function as we were meant to.
>
> *Brown, 2010.*

Most of us know the pain of not belonging. That moment of feeling outside the circle, unsure of our place, sensing that our presence is tolerated rather than welcomed. It is a deeply uncomfortable experience, and one that can linger long after the moment has passed.

I was reminded of this recently at a dinner party I attended with my partner. A small miscommunication meant the hosts were unsure whether I was meant to be there. It was joked about throughout the evening. Comments were made about seating and numbers. Nothing overtly cruel, but enough to make my place in the room feel uncertain.

I didn't know the hosts well. Everyone else shared years of history that I didn't. I had already arrived feeling like an outsider, and instead of being drawn in, I felt exposed. I smiled, joined in, and did what many of us do in those moments. But internally, it was painful.

Neuroscience helps us understand why experiences like this can hurt so much. Research has shown that the brain processes social exclusion in much the same way as it processes physical pain. Functional MRI studies demonstrate that the same regions of the brain, such as the anterior cingulate cortex, activate when we experience rejection or disconnection, just as they do when we experience physical injury (Eisenberger et al., 2003).

Not belonging doesn't just feel bad – it literally hurts.

From an evolutionary perspective, this is quite protective. For most of human history, belonging to a group was essential for survival. Disconnection signalled danger and could very well have been life-threatening. Our nervous systems still carry this ancient alarm system.

But, for anyone impacted by trauma in childhood, that alarm has often been sounding for years. Many have learned, through repeated ruptures, that they are the outsider, the problem, the one who doesn't fit. Some systems designed to protect them unintentionally deepen this wound, particularly when belonging is disrupted through exclusion, displacement or removal.

And some of our workplaces, unfortunately, can mirror these experiences.

When we feel excluded, misunderstood or unsupported at work, the same alarm systems activate. We move into survival mode, doing what we need to do to protect ourselves. And while doing so, our capacity for relational work, the very heart of our roles, becomes compromised.

While my dinner party situation was difficult, it would have felt a whole lot worse if that had happened to me in a staffroom with colleagues I had to see every day.

If not belonging hurts this deeply, it's worth slowing down to understand what belonging actually is, and why it matters so much for our wellbeing.

What is belonging?

Belonging is defined as a core human need; it's the need to feel accepted, valued, connected and held by others (Baumeister & Leary, 1995). Rogers (1951) described belonging as the yearning for positive regard, emotional closeness and connection.

Belonging is less about fitting in and more about being accepted as our authentic selves.

If we look back on my dinner party experience, I was doing my best to fit in, smiling through the jokes, which certainly didn't elicit a sense of belonging. Quite the opposite: I was trying to fit in; I wasn't being authentic.

Belonging also goes beyond being accepted. It includes mattering – feeling that who we are and what we bring actually makes a difference. That our presence counts. That we are not just tolerated, but valued, and that we have something meaningful to contribute.

So, how do we support others to feel like they belong?

One of the best pieces of advice I received in my career came from Sue Nilsen, the principal I worked with in my graduate role as a teacher.

She said, 'There is something likeable in every one of these kids. Some of them will try to make it hard to find that thing, but it is now your job to find it and hold on to it, particularly on the more difficult days.'

It's a piece of advice I have taken with me into every setting and into every interaction with a young person.

This lens makes it much easier to form a positive relationship with these young people, one that encourages them to be their authentic self and be valued for who they are. It's not just beneficial for them, but more sustainable for us, too.

Studies show that foster carers and out-of-home care professionals who genuinely like the children in their care form stronger, more consistent relationships and experience higher levels of compassion satisfaction, a known buffer against compassion fatigue and burnout. Reinhardt (2016) found that carers who believed they were making a positive difference reported greater satisfaction in their roles. Other research similarly highlights that relational connection and a sense of impact are critical in mitigating emotional exhaustion in trauma-exposed work.

When we genuinely like the young people we support, it becomes easier to see their strengths, their potential and their future. It also becomes easier to stay.

We don't often get to see those futures unfold, but now and again, a former student or client reaches out. We get a tiny window into their adult life. The ones who've reached out to me and have built stability, purpose and meaningful relationships seem to share something in common: they found belonging. Somewhere. With someone. In some rhythm of their life, they felt safe, valued and connected. They felt that they mattered.

In my experience, that sense of belonging most often arrived through relationships with adults who kept showing up. Adults who stayed curious. Adults who didn't give up on them when things became difficult.

What is often missed in these conversations is that this way of relating not only benefits children and young people – it sustains the adults who show up for them. When relationships are grounded in genuine regard rather than constant management, they become a source of energy rather than depletion.

Belonging doesn't just change outcomes for the people we support. It shapes whether we can keep doing this work at all.

So, I'll repeat Sue's advice: become a detective for the likeable thing. Look for what matters about each child or young person, especially on the hard days. It will make a difference for them, and it will make this work more sustainable for you.

Of course, there will be days when that feels easier said than done; days when behaviour, stress or systems make it hard to hold on to that likeable thread.

This is where the idea of unconditional positive regard becomes not just helpful, but essential.

Unconditional positive regard

Psychologist Carl Rogers first wrote about the popular concept of unconditional positive regard in 1957. While it emerged from humanistic therapy, its relevance reaches far beyond clinical settings. At its heart, unconditional positive regard is not a technique, but a relational stance – one that can shape how we lead, teach, support and work alongside others.

The idea invites us to meet another human being with complete, non-judgemental acceptance. It means holding someone in positive regard, not because of what they have done or how they are behaving, but because they are a fellow human being.

At its core, unconditional positive regard reminds us that worth is not something that needs to be earned. A person does not become deserving of care once they perform well, regulate perfectly or meet our expectations. They are worthy simply because they are human.

In practice, this means we do not withdraw our care when someone is struggling. We do not offer kindness only when someone performs well, behaves as expected or meets our standards. We do not wait for someone to 'deserve' our compassion. Instead, we meet children, young people, families and colleagues exactly where they are, and offer acceptance alongside clear boundaries.

A common myth of unconditional positive regard is that it means permitting poor behaviour. That is not what the work is about. We do not abandon boundaries or lower expectations. Instead, we separate the person from their behaviour. We refuse to define someone by a difficult moment, and we refuse to give up on their worth, even when their behaviour is challenging.

It may be helpful to break down the principles of unconditional positive regard:

- **Separate the person from their behaviour.** Practise reframing how we think and speak about the way someone is behaving. For example, *They are a nightmare today* becomes *They are struggling to stay regulated today, and I'm finding it difficult.*
- **Take a non-judgemental stance.** Check in with yourself. *Am I bringing any biases into this moment?*
- **Recall knowledge of development.** Consider the impact of stress, adversity and trauma. *What may have happened to this person that led them here?*
- **Remember that people do well when they can.** Stay curious. *I wonder how they are feeling right now? What is getting in the way of them doing well?*
- **Hold belief in growth and change.** Stay committed. *What opportunities would I like to see for them in the future? What will it take to get them there? What support can I provide?*

This takes conscious practice: catching our thoughts, noticing what we say in staffrooms and, of course, supporting the children and young people in our care.

We should also be practising unconditional positive regard with our colleagues.

I'm not going to lie. It is often much easier to practise unconditional positive regard with trauma-impacted young people than it is with adults, particularly colleagues. Many workplace cultures actively discourage it. There is often an unspoken, or sometimes very vocal, belief that adults should know better, that they are paid to be here, and therefore should perform without friction, emotion or support.

It is worth noticing how conditional our regard often becomes in workplaces. When someone meets deadlines, remains polite and keeps their emotions out of meetings, they are often labelled as professional or easy to work with. When someone is quiet, irritable, overwhelmed or cries in the staffroom, they may be met with judgement, discomfort or subtle exclusion.

This way of thinking is reinforced by broader systems that value productivity over humanity and performance over presence. But if we genuinely want trauma-informed, relational workplaces, we need to extend the same grace to adults that we offer to young people.

Adults, just like young people, have nervous systems shaped by their history. They carry stories, stressors, losses, traumas and unmet needs. And while we may not always agree with how someone shows up, we can still choose to regard them as fully human, doing their best in that moment, and worthy of care.

This shift may seem radical. It runs counter to individualistic, performance-driven work cultures. It asks us to prioritise connection over perfection, and to see workplace relationships not as transactions but as shared human experiences.

Boosting belonging and relationships

For adults, belonging at work is not about forced closeness or personality fit. It is about feeling seen, valued, connected and safe enough to be human while doing demanding work. It's a subjective experience, one that comes from our own unique perception. So we can't approach belonging with a one-size-fits-all intervention.

In busy, high-pressure workplaces, especially those shaped by trauma, connection is often the first thing to slip.

The good news is that belonging doesn't require grand gestures. It can be built through small, repeated experiences of being seen, valued and held in relationship. Here are a few ways teams can intentionally strengthen belonging, without adding more to already full plates.

Find that likeable thing in our colleagues, too

It would be remiss of me not to name that the likeable detective approach doesn't stop with children and young people. It can do powerful work in our relationships with colleagues as well.

We don't need to be best friends with everyone we work with. Belonging at work is not about forced closeness or personality fit. But when we intentionally look for the strengths, values and human qualities of the people around us, something shifts. We become more connected, more generous in our interpretations, and far less likely to reduce one another to a single behaviour, moment or role.

This matters in trauma-impacted settings, where stress is high and capacity is often stretched. Under pressure, our nervous systems are more likely to move into threat-based thinking. We become quicker to judge, label or distance ourselves from colleagues who frustrate us, work differently or show up in ways we don't immediately understand. Over time, this erodes trust and belonging.

Actively looking for the likeable thing interrupts that pattern. It might be a colleague's steadiness in a crisis. Their humour when things feel heavy. Their commitment to a particular student or family. Their reliability. Their creativity. Their willingness to ask hard questions. Sometimes the likeable thing is not warm or charismatic; sometimes it's quiet competence, persistence or integrity.

Strengthening relationships through everyday interactions

Belonging is built in small, repeated moments, not big initiatives.

Studies on relational trust in schools show that consistent, respectful day-to-day interactions between adults are among the strongest predictors of staff wellbeing and collective efficacy (Bryk & Schneider, 2002; Louis et al., 2010).

Practical approaches include:

- Leaders greeting staff by name and checking in beyond task-based conversations
- Meetings that begin with brief human connection, not just agendas
- Making space for acknowledgement after difficult work, not only after success.

As you can see, this isn't about adding more to already full workloads – these are micro-moment adjustments that prioritise connection and relationships.

Mentoring and buddy connections within teams

Many of the teams I work with span generations. Early career practitioners bring energy, new ideas and fresh training. More experienced staff bring depth, wisdom and pattern recognition that only comes with time. When these groups are siloed, everyone loses.

Intentional intergenerational connection creates opportunities for learning to flow both ways. Mentoring relationships, peer partnerships or even informal check-ins can help newer staff feel supported while reminding experienced practitioners that their knowledge matters. Research consistently shows that mentoring and collegial relationships are linked to higher job satisfaction, stronger commitment and a greater sense of belonging at work.

This is especially relevant in education and youth sectors, where younger practitioners often bring energy and innovation, while more experienced staff hold institutional memory and relational wisdom (Kram, 1985; Allen et al., 2004).

Practical approaches include:

- Formalising a structured mentoring or buddy system in your work setting
- Co-facilitating learning or projects across career stages
- Reflective practice opportunities
- Valuing lived experience and professional experience as equally legitimate forms of expertise.

Strengths-based approaches

Strengths-based approaches invite us to shift our attention from what is missing or not yet working, to what is already present and capable. Strengths-based approaches in workplaces are associated with higher engagement, lower burnout and increased wellbeing (Niemiec, 2018; Govindji & Linley, 2007). Importantly, they also buffer against compassion fatigue by reconnecting practitioners to meaning and capability.

In teams, this might include:

- Naming and utilising staff strengths intentionally in roles and projects
- Reflective conversations that include 'What helped this go well?'
- Colleagues noticing and naming strengths. These can be the strengths we used to navigate challenging moments or those that we notice about others on a day-to-day basis.

Over time, these practices contribute to a culture where people feel valued and they support a sense of mattering and belonging, both of which are deeply protective in demanding work.

Because strengths-based practice is such a powerful lever for wellbeing, culture and sustainability, we will return to it in much greater depth in chapter 10. We will explore how to identify strengths, embed them into team culture and use them intentionally without bypassing the very real challenges of the work.

Gratitude as a relational practice

Gratitude practices support belonging when they are specific, relational and mutual.

Research shows that gratitude strengthens relationships by reinforcing care, trust and mutual appreciation. When people feel seen and appreciated for what they contribute, not just what they endure, this increases wellbeing, commitment and relational safety within teams. Gratitude also helps counter the natural negativity bias that can develop in high-stress environments, where attention is often (understandably) drawn to risk, problems and what still needs fixing.

What matters most is *how* gratitude is expressed.

Relational gratitude:

- Names specific actions or qualities, rather than giving generic praise
- Acknowledges the effort, care or intention behind the work
- Flows in multiple directions, not only from leaders to staff.

For example, there is a meaningful difference between: 'Thanks everyone for your hard work,' and 'I really appreciated how you stayed with that family yesterday, even when the conversation was difficult.'

In teams, gratitude can be woven into everyday practice in simple ways:

- A shared gratitude wall or board where contributions are named in real time
- Brief check-out questions such as, 'What's something you appreciated about someone today?'
- Leaders and colleagues naming contributions out loud, especially after emotionally demanding work.

Having a voice in the bigger picture

One of the quickest ways to erode belonging is to exclude people from decisions that affect their daily work. When staff have input into strategic plans, wellbeing priorities or ways of working together, they are more likely to feel respected and invested.

This doesn't mean every decision is made by consensus. It means people are consulted, informed and acknowledged. We covered some practical strategies for this in chapters 4 and 5.

None of these belonging interventions work in isolation. Belonging is cumulative. It's built through consistency, not intensity.

We cannot ask people to create belonging for others if they don't experience it themselves.

When teams feel connected, supported and valued, they are far better placed to offer the same to the children, young people and communities they serve.

Belonging, like all trauma-informed work, is part of how we choose to be with each other every day.

Chapter summary

- Consistent, caring relationships can alter life trajectories for young people, but only when the adults offering those relationships are supported to stay.
- Relationships are one of the strongest predictors of wellbeing across the lifespan, acting as stress regulators that protect physical and mental health.
- The pain of not belonging is real, embodied and biologically registered as threat, which can push individuals and teams into survival mode.
- Belonging is not about fitting in, but about being accepted as our authentic selves.
- Unconditional positive regard separates a person's worth from their behaviour while maintaining clear boundaries.
- Belonging at work is built through small, repeated experiences of being seen, valued and included.
- Strong team relationships and cultures of belonging are key reasons practitioners choose to stay in trauma-affected work.

From insight to impact

- **Practise unconditional positive regard with colleagues, not only young people.** Notice where your regard becomes conditional at work. Who is easy to extend grace to, and who isn't? Commit to separating people from behaviour in adult spaces as deliberately as you do in student-facing work, particularly during moments of stress or conflict.
- **Strengthen one relational practice.** Choose one small, repeatable practice that builds connection: a consistent check-in, naming strengths in meetings, mentoring across career stages, or shared gratitude.
- **Find that likeable thing.** Take Sue Nilsen's wise advice and find the likeable thing in each and every child or young person you work with. There will be benefits for them, and for you!

9

Trauma-Informed Leadership and Culture

Leadership is never an easy task. It's even harder when you're leading people working in complex systems who are caring for others. In trauma-affected settings, leadership is about navigating complexity, emotional labour and systems that are often under strain, while still trying to create workplaces where people can function and perform well.

Recent data on the wellbeing of the Australian workforce paints a sobering picture (Australian Bureau of Statistics, 2022; Australian Institute of Health and Welfare, 2022; Gallup Australia, 2023). The findings don't surprise me, but they've been fairly heavily ignored and unaddressed in our modern workplaces.

In a typical team of 20 employees:

- two are living with PTSD or complex PTSD
- three have experienced childhood abuse
- four have had a diagnosed mental health condition in the past year
- three women and one man have experienced intimate partner violence
- three women and one man have experienced sexual violence since age 15
- ten report chronic workplace stress.

If we sit with these numbers for a while, we might start to think of the kind of leadership we would like to offer.

We don't need leaders to become therapists, but we do need leaders who recognise the impact of our experiences, reduce further harm, and work towards creating safe, supportive and healing cultures.

In the NEST framework, trauma-informed leadership sits deeply within *strengthen*. It asks us to strengthen our cultures, our relationships, our communication, our boundaries, our wellbeing systems and our shared language.

What is trauma-informed leadership?

Trauma-informed leadership goes beyond psychological safety and explicitly acknowledges the realities of adversity and harm in the workplace.

Trauma-informed leaders recognise how trauma, stress and chronic pressure shape the way people show up, and embed practices that restore safety, enhance trust and empower the people they are leading. These practices include embodying attributes and behaviours that promote wellbeing and resilience (Lloyd, 2024).

Becoming a trauma-informed leader means broadening our lens. We still centre the operational and strategic aspects of our work, we prioritise the children and young people in our care, and we hold the experiences of our staff and communities as equally important.

This is a radical approach; it moves us beyond traditional styles of leadership and towards more compassionate, human-centred ways of working with our teams. It asks us to consider what kind of workplace we want to create, how we attract good people and how we look after them so they can choose to stay.

This way of leading is grounded in neuroscience, backed by evidence, and offers us a holistic and actionable blueprint for working well together (Koloroutis & Pole, 2021; Robson, 2025).

Trauma-informed leaders are our parent birds of the NEST. They don't just sit above the nest; they actively shape it, protect it, and ensure it can weather storms. They:

- **Notice.** Parent birds are in tune with the environment. In this stage, leaders notice what impacts their people, the stressors, the histories, the patterns and their own nervous systems. They name what's happening without judgement, making the nest safer simply by acknowledging what is real.
- **Embed.** Parent birds don't strengthen the nest once – they weave and re-weave. Leaders embed trauma-informed practice into daily rhythms such as how meetings are run, how conflict is managed, how expectations are communicated and how people are spoken to. Every strand becomes part of the nest's structure.
- **Strengthen.** Here, leaders reinforce the foundations. They help the team hold steady through predictable communication, relational consistency, shared norms and emotionally safe workplaces. A strengthened nest protects everyone inside it and supports their ability to do complex, human-centred work.
- **Thrive.** When the nest is strong, birds can learn to fly. Leaders cultivate spaces where people don't just cope, they grow, create, connect and find meaning. This is where joy returns, belonging deepens and the whole community begins to lift.

We'll explore this approach throughout the rest of the chapter.

What I wish I knew before I led in a trauma-affected environment

When I first stepped into leadership, I carried a very naive assumption: *Adults are easier to lead than young people.*

I had spent over a decade working in alternative settings, immersed in the complexity of trauma-impacted young people. I had grown skilled at seeing beneath behaviour, holding boundaries and practising unconditional positive regard.

Without realising it, I had developed a kind of tunnel vision. I was deeply attuned to students' needs, but far less aware of what was happening for the adults around me.

Just before I stepped into my first leadership role, a mentor shared something powerful with me during a coaching conversation. After years of leading in alternative education, she had noticed that adults who choose this work often present with oppositional behaviours. We laughed a little about how this had shown up in me: in my passion, my stubbornness, my determination to advocate fiercely for students.

What we didn't explore enough at the time was *why*. Why do caring, committed, values-driven adults sometimes present with opposition, defensiveness, reactivity or withdrawal?

Trauma-informed leadership helps us see the fuller picture.

Adults in trauma-affected environments often carry some or all of the following:

- high emotional labour
- chronic workplace stress
- personal histories of adversity
- vicarious trauma
- moral distress
- an ongoing sense of responsibility for the young people they support.

And those statistics I shared earlier of the average Australian team highlight that many of our colleagues are carrying their own experiences of trauma and mental illness.

The behaviours we might see as *difficult* are often stress responses, survival strategies or protective habits shaped over the years. This work can feel difficult to control, but what helps us feel safe is finding something we can control.

Just as with our students, behaviour is communication. And in the adults we lead, it is usually communicating fatigue, fear, overwhelm, unmet needs or a longing for safety and clarity.

My journey into leadership was a baptism by fire

A school I loved was entering a turbulent period, and a new leadership team was needed. The role of Lead Teacher opened, and I stepped towards it with a mix of excitement and grief: excitement for the possibility of making a bigger difference, and grief for the classroom work I adored and wasn't sure I was ready to leave.

But nothing prepared me for the complexity of leading adults who were themselves holding the weight of trauma-impacted work. I quickly learned that:

- Adults can be just as dysregulated as young people
- Oppositional behaviour is often a sign of fear or unmet needs
- Team conflict is a symptom of chronic stress
- People who care deeply can sometimes react intensely
- Culture can either soothe or inflame stress responses.

It takes a lot of work to lead a team through these situations and towards a trauma-informed culture. And, while it's the leader's role to lead the team, we all have our part to play. Leaders alone cannot create a culture of wellbeing.

This chapter is here to support the leadership teams, but everything we unpack will benefit the team members, too, so no matter your role, please read on.

Multi-tiered systems of support (MTSS) for staff wellbeing

In schools, a multi-tiered system of support (MTSS) is a proactive and preventative framework that integrates data and instruction to maximise student success from a strengths-based perspective.

To understand how this might apply when considering the wellbeing of professionals, we'll first explore how MTSS is currently used within schools.

MTSS is an effective way to organise support for students with instruction in the classroom, attendance, behaviour and wellbeing. It's a very useful framework for schools, but is equally useful across other services.

Looking at the school example, MTSS includes three tiers of intensity for instruction and intervention (see figure 6):

- Tier 1 is high-quality, schoolwide programming and supports designed to meet the needs of all students.
- Tier 2 is small-group, standardised interventions that support students who need this level of care and instruction. Tier 2 practices have demonstrated positive effects for desired outcomes and are aligned with student needs.
- Tier 3 is intensive intervention that is individualised based on student need. It is provided to students needing more than Tier 2 interventions and who have ongoing, intensive needs.

It is important to note that students receive Tier 2 or 3 supports *in addition* to Tier 1, not as a replacement.

Figure 6: Multi-tiered system of support (MTSS) framework

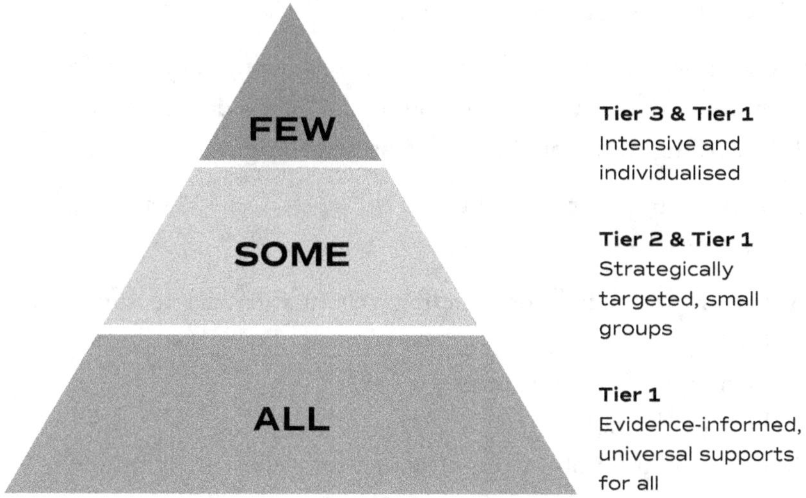

For schools with higher-priority cohorts of students, such as those experiencing socioeconomic disadvantage, learning English as an additional language, or living with additional needs, our attention is often pulled towards Tier 2 and Tier 3 interventions. When needs are visible and urgent, it makes sense that targeted and intensive supports take centre stage.

And yet, as the framework reminds us, Tier 1 is the foundation. These are the universal supports we provide to *all* students to create the conditions for learning. The stronger and more intentional our Tier 1 supports are, the fewer students we expect to require Tier 2 and Tier 3 interventions.

This same thinking can help us reframe how we approach staff wellbeing. Rather than responding only when someone is already struggling, burning out or on the brink of leaving, we can view staff wellbeing through a similar multi-tiered lens – one that invites us to think collectively, rather than individually, about how care, support and responsibility are shared across a system.

Importantly, this does not mean leaders are expected to *be* the support at every tier. Trauma-informed leadership is not about doing everything yourself. It is about noticing risk, building strong universal foundations, and working alongside wellbeing teams and external supports to ensure the right help is available at the right time.

Before reading on, it may be helpful to pause and reflect on how wellbeing is currently held in your setting. You might like to do this on your own, with a leadership team, or alongside trusted colleagues.

Start by sketching your pyramid with the labels Tier 1, Tier 2 and Tier 3. Then ask yourselves:

- What are we already doing effectively at each tier to support staff wellbeing?
- Which supports are clear and accessible?
- Where are the gaps?
- Who carries most of the responsibility for wellbeing right now?

Holding this reflection as we move through the tiers can help ground the framework in your real context.

In Tier 1, we include the evidence-based proactive strategies to support wellbeing and reduce stress across the team, including things like:

- trauma-informed training to ensure staff competency
- onboarding processes that set new staff members up for success
- role clarity and service clarity
- regulation practices that are embedded in our ways of working
- workload that is reasonable and appropriate
- team connection and culture that is prioritised and co-created.

In Tier 2, we would recognise that some situations require targeted interventions to support staff. These supports may include things like:

- debriefing and defusing after critical incidents
- reflective practice conversations
- group supervision
- further professional learning and development
- formalised mentoring
- check-in and check-out practices.

In Tier 3, we have individualised and intensive support for staff to navigate crises and periods of high stress. These supports may include:

- Employee Access Program (EAP)
- crisis support services
- time to access private counselling services.

Looking at staff wellbeing through a trauma-informed lens reminds us that our leadership sits in establishing a strong Tier 1 approach. This involves co-creating shared norms, rhythms and supports with our teams so that every staff member, including those of us in leadership, is set up for success and held by a culture where wellbeing is part of the work, not an added extra.

From there, our role is to notice when additional layers of support are needed, and to normalise their use as part of a healthy system.

When leaders openly name, model and encourage the use of these supports, including for ourselves, we reduce shame and reinforce the idea that wellbeing takes intentional work.

Practising what we preach

In trauma-affected settings, it is easy for leaders to slip into survival mode without even realising it. We spend our days holding space for others, responding to crises, supporting staff, navigating complexity and absorbing the emotional labour of a whole community. Urgency becomes normalised; self-sacrifice is celebrated.

But if we are not well, we cannot lead well.

When leaders do not model wellbeing as an ongoing practice, something we actively tend to rather than an ideal state we magically reach, teams can begin to draw unhelpful conclusions. Stress starts to feel like a personal failure rather than a human response to demanding work. Needing support can feel like incompetence instead of reality.

For a long time, I believed my team would benefit most from my unwavering steadiness, my capacity to stay composed under pressure, and my ability to hold space when others needed support. There is certainly value in this, but my leadership was missing something vital.

That became clear during a conversation with a teacher that I have never forgotten.

I was facilitating a team debrief following a difficult incident with a student. We worked through what happened, supported the student and checked that the staff involved had the wellbeing supports they needed. After the debrief, a teacher approached me and asked how I managed to be so unaffected by the critical incidents and disclosures we navigate as a school. She commented that I always appeared calm and steady.

By that point, I had been working in trauma-affected settings for many years. We *do* build capacity. The work becomes more familiar and, in some ways, less shocking. But what I realised in that moment was this: my calm had been interpreted as effortlessness.

What was missing from my leadership was vulnerability.

I was not sharing with my team when I found things difficult, or what I was doing behind the scenes in order to keep showing up. By staying silent about my own process, I wasn't normalising theirs, and our culture of caring for each other was limited as a result. That realisation shifted how I thought about modelling wellbeing.

Let's take a look at some aspects of leadership that land very differently when we practise them, not just preach them.

Emotional intelligence

Trauma-informed leadership requires emotional intelligence. This means tuning in to what is happening within us, understanding how it affects the people around us, and responding with intention rather than reactivity (Goleman, 2006).

When leaders are honest about their emotions, acknowledge challenges and communicate with care, they create cultures where it is safe for others to do the same.

Awareness of our nervous systems and stress response

In leadership roles, our nervous systems are constantly in conversation with others' nervous systems. When we are overwhelmed, rushed or dysregulated, that state does not stay contained within us. It shapes the tone of meetings, the way we speak to others, the decisions we make and the team's emotional climate. Stress spreads quickly, particularly in environments already shaped by trauma.

Leaders who lead from stress compromise their decision-making, their capacity to respond strategically and their ability to create regulation in their teams. Awareness helps us interrupt the pattern.

When we understand our own nervous system and stress responses, we can recognise when we are moving towards survival mode and intervene before we get there.

Self-regulation

Self-regulation enables leaders to manage their emotions in ways that support clearer thinking and healthier team dynamics. This could look like setting aside small pockets of time for grounding practices, such as deep breathing or mindfulness at the start or end of the day, or taking a brief moment to steady yourself before entering a challenging conversation.

By weaving these practices into our daily routines, we create a consistent sense of emotional balance that supports effective decision-making, strengthens relationships and helps us lead with intention rather than reactivity.

The irony is that most of us in leadership positions already know this. We talk about regulation with our teams. We teach it to young people. We name its importance in trauma-informed practice. And yet, we are often the first to abandon these practices for ourselves, dismissing them in the face of busyness, urgency or the belief that there simply isn't time.

But when leaders consistently override their own regulation needs, the cost eventually shows up in our bodies, in our relationships and in the cultures we are trying to build.

A proactive approach to wellbeing

Trauma-informed leadership is not reactive; it is preventative. It recognises that wellbeing is not something we tend to once people are already burnt out, overwhelmed or leaving our workplace. It is something we build and protect along the way.

A proactive approach to wellbeing might include engaging in supervision or reflective practice, setting and modelling clear boundaries around work hours, or being part of a community of practice that offers peer support and shared language. These practices are not indulgent; they are protective.

Most importantly, we must talk about these practices. When leaders openly name the ways they care for themselves, it signals that wellbeing is part of the job. It becomes a cultural norm, shaping a workplace where everyone feels permitted to take care of themselves too.

Turning difficult conversations into human conversations

Difficult conversations are an unavoidable part of leadership, particularly in trauma-affected environments. They are the conversations where behaviour needs to be addressed, boundaries clarified, concerns raised or decisions explained. They might be with staff, parents or carers, external professionals or young people.

These conversations often carry weight far beyond the immediate issue. They can feel charged, uncomfortable, or emotionally risky both for the person leading the conversation and for those on the receiving end.

Conversations carry history, emotion, power and meaning. By the time someone is sitting across from a leader, they may already be carrying stress, fear, shame or a sense of being judged. Many parents, carers, and staff in trauma-affected systems bring their own experiences of school trauma, system harm or previous negative encounters with authority.

As leaders, we bring things too: Time pressure. Responsibility. Fatigue. The weight of holding risk and accountability for others. When these layers collide, conversations can quickly move into survival mode.

When people are stressed or dysregulated, their capacity for reflection, collaboration and problem-solving is reduced. This is not a lack of willingness or competence. It is a nervous system doing its best to protect. Trauma-informed leadership asks us to account for this reality, rather than pushing through it.

It may be helpful to reflect on your difficult conversations and see what comes up:

- Which conversations do I find difficult?
- Who are they with?
- What happens in my body as I anticipate having the conversation?

We're now going to unpack some ideas that may support us in leading these conversations.

Leading with regulation

One of the most common mistakes leaders make is trying to get through a difficult conversation without first attending to regulation – both theirs and the other person's.

When someone is highly stressed, fearful or dysregulated, their capacity to take in information, reflect or problem-solve is limited. The same is true for leaders.

Supporting regulation doesn't require anything elaborate. Often, it's about slowing the pace, choosing the right environment and signalling safety. This might look like:

- taking a moment to ground yourself before the conversation
- greeting the person at the entrance or walking side-by-side to get to an appropriate room (consider noise level and environment)
- offering them a glass of water (lowers cortisol)
- having sensory tools available in the room (these are not just for kids)
- allowing them to sit closest to the door (easy exit if they need to leave)
- asking them what they need before you begin
- naming the purpose of the conversation clearly and calmly.

These small actions can shift a conversation from adversarial to human.

Being mindful of power

Leadership conversations are never neutral. Whether we intend it or not, our role carries authority. For some people, that authority is linked to past experiences of being silenced, punished or not believed. For others, it may bring fear about consequences, judgement or loss of control.

We can acknowledge the power imbalance and work carefully to empower the other person. This means:

- being transparent about our role and responsibilities
- looking to them as someone we can learn from and offer support to
- avoiding language that positions us as the sole decision-maker when collaboration is possible.

Recognising people as experts in their own experience

One of the most powerful shifts leaders can make in difficult conversations is this: moving from *fixing* to *listening*.

Parents, carers, staff and young people are experts in their own lives. When we position ourselves as curious rather than corrective, people are more likely to engage, reflect and collaborate.

This doesn't mean handing over responsibility or abandoning professional judgement. It means holding a stance of respect. You might say:

- You know this situation better than anyone. What do you think would help?
- What has worked in the past that could help now?
- I'd love to hear your ideas so I can better support you.
- What can we do to make this better?

When people feel seen and heard, conversations become less adversarial and more constructive.

Leading systems change

Any time we work in trauma-informed ways, we are not just supporting individuals – we are changing how people experience the system around them.

For many children, young people, families and staff, the system itself has been the source of harm. Schools, health services, justice systems and welfare organisations are often where people first felt judged, silenced, excluded or unsafe. Trauma-informed leadership asks us to hold this truth, even when it is uncomfortable, and even when we care deeply about the systems we work within.

Systems do not change simply because one person is kind, skilled or well-intentioned. Systems change when patterns shift. When expectations shift. When policies, procedures and everyday practices begin to align with what we now know about trauma, stress and human behaviour.

This is why trauma-informed practice cannot live only at the level of individual interactions or one-off professional learning. Research consistently shows that trauma-informed approaches are most effective when they are implemented at a systems level, rather than as isolated training or individual practice change (Harris & Fallot, 2001; SAMHSA, 2014; Bowen & Murshid, 2016).

For leaders, this means we are not only asking, 'How do I support this person right now?' We are also asking harder, broader questions:

- What in our system is making this harder than it needs to be?
- What are we unintentionally reinforcing through our routines, responses or rules?
- Where are we asking people to adapt to unsafe systems, rather than adapting systems to human needs?

These questions often lead us straight to our policies and procedures.

On paper, many organisations already value safety, respect and wellbeing. But in practice, policies can sometimes prioritise compliance over care, punishment over learning and individual responsibility over shared accountability. They can increase fear, surveillance or hypervigilance, particularly for people who already feel vulnerable within systems.

Trauma-informed leadership invites us to look at policies not just as documents, but as lived experiences. To ask how they feel in the body. To notice whether they create clarity or confusion, predictability or threat, safety or shame.

When policies are trauma-informed, they are clear, transparent and predictable. They reduce unnecessary threat, acknowledge power and include pathways for support, not just consequences. They are applied consistently rather than reactively, and they make space for repair when things go wrong.

Importantly, they are not designed *for* people without them. They are reviewed and shaped with the people most impacted by them. Co-design is not a buzzword here; it is a practical mechanism for safety, trust and shared ownership.

Systems change does not always require sweeping reform. More often, it begins with small, consistent shifts in how decisions are made, how responsibility is shared, and how people are treated when things get messy. It's relational work and over time, those shifts accumulate.

When leaders align values, policies and everyday practices, trauma-informed work stops being an initiative or a checkbox. It becomes how things are done around here. And when that happens, the experience of the system itself begins to heal.

Across this chapter, we have explored leadership as something deeply relational. Something that lives in nervous systems, conversations, boundaries and everyday practices.

And while leadership roles carry particular influence, none of this work happens in isolation. Culture is co-created. Systems shift through collective effort. The nest holds because many strands are woven together.

Chapter summary

- Trauma-informed leadership recognises that many people in our workplaces are carrying personal histories of adversity, chronic stress and exposure to others' trauma, whether or not this is visible.
- Trauma-informed leadership sits within *strengthen* in the NEST framework, strengthening cultures, relationships, communication, boundaries and wellbeing systems so teams can weather pressure over time.
- A multi-tiered approach to staff wellbeing helps leaders move from reactive support to proactive, shared responsibility, with strong universal foundations (Tier 1) supported by targeted and intensive options when needed (Tiers 2 and 3).
- Trauma-informed leadership requires emotional intelligence, nervous system awareness and self-regulation, recognising that stress spreads quickly through teams and so does calm.
- Difficult conversations are inevitable in leadership roles, particularly in trauma-affected systems. When leaders prioritise regulation, acknowledge power and approach conversations with curiosity rather than control, those conversations become more relational and productive.
- Trauma-informed leadership is systems work. It asks leaders to examine how policies, procedures and decision-making processes shape people's experience of the system itself.

From insight to impact

- **Strengthen Tier 1 support.** With your leadership team, map what currently sits at Tier 1 for staff wellbeing. Choose one Tier 1 practice to strengthen or embed more intentionally.
- **Model the wellbeing you want others to practise.** Share, appropriately, how you regulate, set boundaries or seek support. When leaders name their own processes, wellbeing becomes part of the culture rather than a private struggle.
- **Slow down difficult conversations and lead with regulation.** Identify one conversation you have been avoiding or rushing through. Before engaging, check in with your body and prepare for regulation, for yourself and the other person. Approach the conversation with curiosity, recognising the other person as an expert in their own experience.
- **Review one system through a trauma-informed lens.** Choose one policy, procedure or routine that regularly creates tension or distress. Make one small adjustment that increases clarity, fairness or support.

Part IV

Thrive

thrive *verb*
to grow, develop, or be successful.

Cambridge Dictionary

Trauma-informed practice is not only about reducing harm, it's about creating the conditions for growth, purpose and joy. In this final stage, we move beyond survival, drawing from the science of wellbeing and positive psychology. We focus on strengths, belonging, connection and meaning. We imagine what it looks like when individuals, teams and systems don't just cope, but truly thrive.

10

Beyond Baseline: Using Science to Enhance Our Wellbeing

Welcome to the final chapter of *Beyond Survival Mode*. In this chapter, we dive deeper into the science of wellbeing, exploring how we can develop skills, resources and supports that help us move beyond baseline and towards experiences of flourishing.

You might recall that in chapter 1 we unpacked the dual continua model of mental health, highlighting that mental illness and wellbeing are two related, but distinct, concepts. In this chapter, our focus shifts squarely to wellbeing.

My hope is that by the end of this chapter, you will have identified a few practices you can add to your toolkit to intentionally support and enhance your wellbeing as a trauma-informed professional.

What is positive psychology?

> Positive psychology is the scientific study of what makes life worth living.
>
> *Peterson, 2008.*

When Martin Seligman was appointed president of the American Psychological Association in 1998, he introduced the subfield of positive psychology, calling for a greater focus on strengths rather than deficits, and building the good in life rather than only repairing the bad. This created a significant shift within psychology and invited many of us to shift our personal perspective, too.

The field of positive psychology grew quickly. Thousands of researchers around the world have contributed to this area, exploring the core concepts of flourishing, positive emotions, character strengths and relationships, and have developed a wide range of positive psychology interventions to enhance wellbeing.

Over time, these interventions have been adapted for individuals, workplaces, communities and whole systems.

In this chapter, we are going to explore a handful of positive psychology interventions, but before we do, we need to know about our negativity bias.

Negativity bias

Do you ever find yourself scanning through positive feedback you've received, only to look for, and fixate on, the one piece of constructive feedback?

Do you feel fear more strongly than you feel happiness?

Do you notice a young person behaving disruptively before you notice the ten who are settled and on task?

If you answered yes to any of these questions, you are a very normal human being.

What is a negativity bias?

Negativity bias is a well-documented cognitive tendency where negative experiences, information or emotions have a greater impact on us than positive ones of equal intensity. In simple terms, we notice the bad more easily than the good, remember it more vividly and react to it more strongly (Baumeister et al., 2001).

Even when something positive and something negative are objectively similar in magnitude, our emotional and physiological response is often amplified in response to the negative. As humans, we are wired to attend to, learn from and prioritise negative information because, historically, it helped keep us alive (Rozin & Royzman, 2001).

Why is this a good thing?

This function is believed to be part of our evolutionary development. Thousands of years ago, humans lived in environments where threats were immediate and often life-threatening. Missing a sign of danger could mean injury or death, whereas missing a positive experience carried far less risk. Being alert to danger supported survival. We evolved nervous systems that constantly scanned the environment, ready to fight, flee or freeze when needed. And for a long time, that worked.

Negativity bias also plays an important role in early development. Infants and young children have limited experience to draw on, so strong reactions to negative or painful experiences help them learn quickly what to avoid. Research suggests that negative experiences are encoded more rapidly and more deeply than positive ones, particularly early in life (Vaish et al., 2008).

A single frightening or painful moment, such as touching something hot or being startled by a loud noise, can shape future behaviour after just one exposure. This rapid learning supports early risk management, long before language or reasoning skills are fully developed.

But what does our negativity bias mean for us beyond our early development and beyond the daily environmental threats our ancestors experienced?

It's not always a good thing

Negativity bias impacts the way we make decisions and our levels of motivation, and can compromise our wellbeing. While it once served as a function to keep us alive, our negativity bias can be inhibiting our experiences in our current world.

When our negativity bias is constantly activated, our world becomes smaller. Our thinking narrows, our nervous systems stay alert, and our capacity for creativity and connection reduces. We focus on problems, risks and what needs fixing. This can be useful in moments of genuine danger, but costly when it becomes our default state.

For most of us, daily life no longer involves predators or exposure to the elements. Instead, it involves full inboxes, performance pressures, systemic stress, and constant exposure to information through digital and media platforms.

Unfortunately, news and media outlets tend to capitalise on our negativity bias. We are more likely to click on, remember and emotionally react to bad news, which reinforces cycles of fear and hypervigilance. While this can feel like 'staying informed', research shows that chronic exposure to negative news increases stress and anxiety without improving our actual safety (Garfin et al., 2020).

In trauma-affected professions, this effect is often amplified. Educators, youth justice workers, health professionals and community workers are regularly exposed to negative narratives about their industries, alongside daily exposure to distress, risk and crisis. If you are currently finding joy or meaning in your work, it can take intentional effort to protect that joy in the face of constant negativity.

Problem-focused thinking in trauma-affected settings

Understanding our negativity bias gives us helpful insight into why our brains are wired to notice problems. In trauma-affected workplaces, this tendency becomes even more pronounced. We aren't simply noticing negative events; we are often working in systems where stress, uncertainty, emotional labour and risk are part of everyday life. Our brain responds by narrowing its focus and zooming in on what feels urgent or unsafe.

This can create a culture of problem-focused thinking:

- noticing what is going wrong before what is going well
- remembering the most challenging moments of the day
- replaying difficult interactions

- planning for risk more than possibility
- assuming worst-case scenarios.

In the long-term, a constant problem-focused state can limit creativity, hope and collective morale. It can make teams feel stuck in survival mode. And it can make solutions feel impossible.

The good news is that we can practise challenging our negativity bias with exercises like engaging in solutions-focused thinking. This helps us move from 'What is the problem here?' to 'What would it take for things to improve?'

Some examples:

- 'What is causing the teacher shortage?' becomes 'What would help teachers stay and thrive?'
- 'Why are they being so difficult today?' becomes 'What might they need to feel safe and to engage today?'

Solutions-focused thinking doesn't dismiss reality, and it doesn't ignore the problem. It simply opens the door to a wider range of possibilities. Let's try it.

Consider a problem (or problems) that you are currently dealing with. Then:

- Write down your problem.
- Rephrase the language to direct your attention to the solution.
- Brainstorm some possible solutions.

The reality is that we actually have more positive experiences than we are aware of; we just do not feel them as intensely as our negative experiences. When we intentionally notice positive moments, we feel positive emotions.

And this shift is made much easier once we understand what positive emotions can do for our brain and body, which is where we turn next.

Emotions as messages

Emotions are defined as 'a complex reaction pattern, involving experiential, behavioural, and physiological elements, through which an individual attempts to deal with a personally significant matter or event' (American Psychological Association, n.d.).

A widely accepted view is that some emotions are good and others are bad. This is a framing that shows up in everyday language, workplaces and even wellbeing conversations. This view makes intuitive sense because emotions can feel pleasant or deeply uncomfortable. But we know that human experience is far more complex than 'good' or 'bad'.

Take sadness for example. Is sadness a 'bad' emotion? Nobody wants to feel sadness, of course. But sadness shows up when something matters: losing a loved one; a friend moving away; a chapter ending. Sadness is a human response to a difficult situation, a messenger that lets us know something meaningful has been lost or changed and needs tending to.

The importance of sadness was depicted so beautifully in the Pixar film *Inside Out*. We saw Joy try to override Sadness and take away her control in headquarters, resulting in chaos and disconnection in Riley's life. However, when Sadness was allowed to step forward, Riley experienced moments of meaning-making and connection with others, even forming core memories.

When we take a trauma-informed lens, this becomes even more important. Big emotions in response to big experiences are human and expected. When we understand this, we can offer ourselves a little more compassion and begin to see our emotions not as problems to fix, but as messages from a system that is trying hard to keep us safe.

If we step away from judging emotions as good or bad, we can still recognise that some emotions simply feel easier to sit with than others. Some create more space in our bodies, more openness in our thinking and more warmth in our relationships.

These are the emotions Barbara Fredrickson (1998) refers to as 'positive emotions', because they tend to feel pleasant, expansive and supportive of growth. In the next section, we will explore these emotions and the science behind why they matter, especially in the context of trauma-informed wellbeing.

Positive emotions and positive experiences

When I began my Master of Applied Positive Psychology (MAPP), I felt a quiet resistance to the idea of positive emotions. I was worried the science might be fluffy, simplistic or disconnected from the real challenges people face. I imagined the hard sell of 'just feel happy and everything will be okay', which feels both unhelpful and unrealistic, particularly when working alongside people impacted by trauma.

But I was pleasantly surprised when I encountered the work of Dr Barbara Fredrickson. Her research on positive emotions is rigorous, grounded and genuinely transformative. It has since become one of my favourite pieces of the wellbeing science puzzle, and one that many helping professionals come to appreciate once they understand its depth.

Broaden-and-build theory

At the heart of Barbara Fredrickson's work is the broaden-and-build theory. This theory explains why positive emotions matter and how they support our long-term wellbeing, particularly in the context of trauma-informed work.

Positive emotions broaden

When we experience a positive emotion such as joy, hope, gratitude, love, interest, pride or amusement, our scope of attention, thinking and action broadens. We shift into a more open and flexible state, becoming more receptive to new ideas, information and possibilities. This is in contrast to what happens under stress, where our focus narrows towards threat and survival (Fredrickson, 2004).

Positive emotions leave us freer to be creative, curious, playful and experimental. From these behaviours flow opportunities to gain new physical, social and intellectual resources.

This broadening effect shows up in everyday ways. For example:

- Joy in children often leads to play, which then builds physical, cognitive and social skills (Boulton & Smith, 1992; Dolhinow & Bishop, 1970).

- Interest encourages exploration and learning, expanding knowledge and understanding.
- Love strengthens bonding and helps build social resources such as trust and connection.
- Feeling upbeat or energised can increase motivation to exercise, supporting physical resources such as health and strength.

Positive emotions build

Over time, these broadened states begin to accumulate. They do not just feel good in the moment; they help us build durable resources that remain long after the emotion itself has passed (Fredrickson, 2004).

Through repeated experiences of positive emotion, we gradually build:

- physical resources, such as strength, energy and cardiovascular health
- social resources, including relationships, trust and belonging
- intellectual resources, such as knowledge, skills and creativity
- cognitive resources, including flexibility, problem-solving and learning
- psychological resources, such as resilience, optimism and emotional regulation.

These are not small or superficial gains. They become part of our wellbeing scaffolding, the inner and outer resources we draw on during times of stress, adversity and challenge.

The undoing effect

Positive emotions can also help us recover from the physiological impact of stress. Fredrickson describes this as the *undoing effect*, where positive emotions help calm the nervous system, lower heart rate and blood pressure and restore a broader, more flexible state of attention. This is particularly important in trauma-informed work, where stress systems can be chronically activated and recovery time is often limited.

The mechanisms underlying the broaden-and-build theory are grounded in neuroplasticity – the brain's capacity to change in response to repeated experience. When certain emotional states are activated frequently and intentionally, they can contribute to longer-term changes in how we respond to the world.

Over time, this may lead to what researchers describe as a shift in affective style, where openness, flexibility and emotional regulation become more accessible, rather than fleeting states. This does not mean life becomes free of stress or difficulty, but it does suggest that cultivating positive emotions can support greater capacity, steadiness and wellbeing over time.

Rituals and routines to enhance positive emotion

As educators, carers and practitioners, we are often deeply attuned to the emotional experiences of those we support. We notice their distress, respond to their needs, and work hard to create moments of safety, regulation, and connection for them. In the process, it is easy to overlook our own emotional experiences and the wellbeing of the adults around us.

Yet our wellbeing is strengthened not through grand gestures, but through small, intentional moments that evoke positive emotion, both individually and collectively. In trauma-exposed work, these moments are not indulgent or optional. They are protective. They help counterbalance chronic stress, widen our perspective and build the emotional and relational resources we need to keep showing up.

Rituals and routines give positive emotions somewhere to land. When they are woven into the rhythms of our day, they begin to challenge our negativity bias and create cultures that are more sustaining, humane and connected.

Collective practices with colleagues

What went well today, and why?

One of the simplest and most effective practices is asking, 'What went well today, and why?' This question gently shifts attention towards positive moments that might otherwise go unnoticed. Research from positive psychology shows that regularly reflecting on what has gone well supports positive emotion, reinforces competence and strengthens meaning, particularly in high-stress environments (Seligman et al., 2005; Fredrickson, 2001).

When used regularly, in staff rooms, meetings or informal conversations, this question helps rebalance our focus and reminds us that even on hard days, there are moments of competence, care and connection.

Strengths spotting

Another powerful practice is strengths spotting. Noticing and naming the strengths we see in one another builds trust, reinforces positive identity and deepens connection within teams.

Research shows that strengths-based approaches are associated with higher engagement, improved wellbeing and lower burnout (Govindji & Linley, 2007; Niemiec, 2018). When strengths are recognised by others, they also reinforce positive identity and foster trust within teams. This is particularly important in environments where stress can narrow attention towards what is not working.

We will explore strengths more deeply later in this chapter, but even small moments of strengths spotting can shift team culture over time.

Shared humour

Shared humour also plays an important role in trauma-informed workplaces. Laughter is a natural stress regulator. It helps release tension, builds connection, and creates brief moments of relief in otherwise demanding days. Humour does not minimise the seriousness of the work; it helps us stay human within it.

Gratitude

Gratitude, when offered genuinely, supports both the giver and the receiver. Gratitude practices have been consistently linked to improved mood, reduced stress, stronger relationships and enhanced wellbeing (Emmons & McCullough, 2003; Wood et al., 2010). In workplace settings, gratitude also contributes to trust, morale and relational safety over time (Algoe, 2012).

This might look like a gratitude board in the staff room, a handwritten note or a simple verbal acknowledgement. Over time, these small acts help shape a culture where people feel seen and appreciated.

Positive resonance (the science of love)

Don't worry, this isn't about having romantic relationships with our colleagues – but it is about the micro-moments of connection that happen when two people share warmth, attunement or kindness.

A smile, eye contact or a warm greeting can create measurable shifts in our physiology, and are associated with physiological benefits including vagal tone and cardiovascular health (Fredrickson, 2013; Fredrickson & Algoe, 2012). These moments may be brief, but they matter deeply for wellbeing, particularly in environments shaped by stress.

Individual practices

Alongside collective rituals, individual practices also play an important role in enhancing positive emotion.

Savouring

Savouring is the intentional process of attending to, appreciating and enhancing positive experiences. In trauma-exposed work, this matters because our brains are often quick to move past positive moments and return to scanning for threat. Savouring helps slow that process down, allowing positive emotions to register more fully and build over time.

Research describes savouring as occurring across three time orientations: anticipatory savouring, present-moment savouring and reminiscent (or retrospective) savouring (Bryant & Veroff, 2007; Bryant, 2021). Each plays a slightly different role in supporting wellbeing.

Anticipatory savouring involves consciously looking forward to a positive experience. This might be noticing a sense of anticipation about an upcoming walk, a planned holiday or time with someone you enjoy. Anticipation itself can generate positive emotion and give the nervous system something supportive to orient towards, particularly in demanding or stressful periods.

Present-moment savouring refers to fully inhabiting a positive experience as it is happening. This might involve pausing to notice a moment of connection with a student, the satisfaction of completing a task or shared laughter with a colleague. Present-moment savouring asks us to slow down to register the experience in our body, rather than rushing past it.

Reminiscent savouring involves intentionally revisiting positive experiences after they have occurred. This could include reflecting on a meaningful moment, writing it down or sharing it with someone else. Looking back on positive experiences helps reinforce their emotional impact and supports memory consolidation.

All three forms of savouring help extend the benefits of positive emotion beyond fleeting moments. Rather than relying on brief spikes of feeling good, savouring supports the accumulation of emotional and psychological resources over time.

For practitioners working in trauma-affected settings, this can be a gentle yet powerful way to widen attention, restore balance and support sustainable wellbeing.

What went well journalling

What went well journalling builds on the notion of savouring. Writing down positive moments, whether in a journal or on a sticky note, helps train our attention towards enjoyment, effort and success. Over time, this practice can gently shift our perspective and counterbalance the brain's tendency to fixate on what went wrong.

Gratitude journalling

Gratitude journalling directs our attention towards what is supportive, meaningful or sustaining in our lives. When we name what we are grateful for and take time to reflect on why it matters, we interrupt the brain's default tendency to scan for threat and difficulty.

Research consistently shows that gratitude practices are associated with improved mood, reduced stress and stronger relationships (Emmons & McCullough, 2003; Wood et al., 2010). Over time, this practice has been shown to strengthen social bonds, increase feelings of connection and support, and enhance overall psychological wellbeing (Algoe, 2012; Wood et al., 2010).

Play

If languishing is a feeling of aimlessness, emptiness and lack of vitality, then play may be one of its most effective antidotes. In my conversation with Corey Keyes, he described play as an essential wellbeing 'vitamin', something that actively supports our capacity to move beyond survival mode and re-engage with life in more energised and meaningful ways.

Importantly, play in adulthood does not need to look like games or structured activities, although it can. Adult play often shows up in more subtle, relational and creative forms. This might include:

- engaging in creative activities such as drawing, writing, music or crafting without concern for outcome or productivity
- moving the body in ways that feel enjoyable rather than goal-driven, such as dancing, swimming, hiking or playful movement
- sharing humour and lightness with others, including storytelling, joking or playful banter
- immersing ourselves in activities that spark curiosity or absorption, such as puzzles, learning something new or tinkering
- spending time in nature in ways that invite wonder, exploration or sensory engagement.

What matters is not the activity itself, but the quality of the experience. Play is characterised by a sense of freedom, enjoyment and intrinsic motivation. It is chosen for the pleasure and vitality it brings, not because it is productive or useful.

Research suggests that play supports wellbeing by increasing positive emotion, enhancing creativity, strengthening social bonds and restoring psychological flexibility (Brown, 2009; van der Kolk, 2014). For adults working in trauma-affected systems, these benefits are not luxuries. They are protective factors that help us stay connected to ourselves and others, even in the midst of complexity.

Play also reconnects us with parts of ourselves that can become lost under the weight of responsibility. It reminds us that we are more than our roles, our workloads or our capacity to cope. In doing so, it supports not just our individual wellbeing, but our ability to bring warmth, presence and humanity into the spaces where we work.

Positive experiences and positive emotions are not just nice additions to our lives. They are central to our capacity to enhance our own wellbeing and to support the wellbeing of those around us. With this foundation in place, we now turn to the science of character strengths, and how identifying and using our strengths can further support us to move beyond survival mode.

From what's wrong to what's strong

Trauma-informed practice teaches us to move from asking 'What's wrong with you?' to 'What happened to you?', a shift that invites compassion, curiosity and understanding. This is the heart of *notice* in the NEST framework: slowing down to see the context, the patterns and the story beneath the behaviour. It helps us build psychological and relational safety, and it lays the foundation for meaningful change.

But as we move into this final stage, *thrive*, we visit and expand the other side of the coin: understanding what has happened is not the end of the story.

When we have been traumatised or chronically stressed, we often carry heavy narratives about who we are – stories shaped by fear, shame or a sense of not being good enough. These internal narratives are frequently reinforced when our stress-based behaviours lead to exclusion, misunderstanding or disconnection from others.

In *thrive*, we begin to explore how we can reclaim a more empowering narrative – one that does not deny what has been hard, but also recognises the strengths, values, and qualities that have helped us survive, adapt, care, persist and keep showing up.

So, building on 'What happened to you?', we now include a different question: 'What's strong within you?'

One of the most robust and well-researched ways we can do this is through the VIA Character Strengths (see www.viacharacter.org).*

Values in action: the VIA Character Strengths

Developed by Dr Christopher Peterson and Dr Martin Seligman, the VIA Classification of Character Strengths is the result of a large-scale international research project. The aim was to identify the strengths that appear across cultures, religions, languages and historical contexts.

What the researchers found was striking. Twenty-four character strengths consistently appeared: qualities that humans everywhere recognise as central to how we live, relate, connect, and contribute. These strengths were named VIA, standing for Values in Action.

The 24 strengths are grouped into six broader domains:

- **Wisdom**, including curiosity, creativity and love of learning
- **Courage**, including bravery, perseverance and honesty
- **Humanity**, including kindness, love and social intelligence
- **Justice**, including fairness, teamwork and leadership
- **Temperance**, including self-regulation, forgiveness and prudence
- **Transcendence**, including gratitude, hope, humour and appreciation of beauty.

Together, these strengths offer a shared language for describing what is right with us. They name the qualities that shape who we are, beyond our roles, job titles or achievements.

Each of us has *signature strengths*: the strengths we draw on most naturally and consistently. When we use them, they tend to feel energising and authentic. They are the parts of us that feel most 'us', and in complex or trauma-exposed work, they can become steadying anchors.

I have leaned on my own strengths consistently throughout my time in this work. I draw on my strength of appreciation of beauty when I head out for a long walk in nature after a stressful day. I lean into humour when connecting with young people, allowing their humour to energise me in return. And I rely on social intelligence when navigating the complexity of supporting a room full of trauma-impacted young people.

What I can see now, with the benefit of hindsight and the research to support it, is that these moments were benefiting my wellbeing and deepening my resources. They helped me experience positive emotion alongside stress, stay connected to meaning in the work, and feel more like myself rather than consumed by the role. They softened the impact of difficult days and reminded me of what I brought into the space.

This personal experience aligns closely with what the research tells us. When we intentionally notice and use our strengths, we tend to experience more positive emotion, deeper engagement, stronger relationships and a greater sense of meaning and accomplishment (Niemiec & McGrath, 2019; Niemiec, 2018; Biswas-Diener et al., 2011). Strengths use can reduce the impact of challenging experiences by creating a more balanced internal narrative, one that holds both challenge and capacity.

Importantly, the benefits of strengths-based approaches extend beyond individuals. When strengths are recognised and supported within teams, communication improves, collaboration deepens and collective problem-solving becomes more effective. Stress reduces, coping systems stabilise, and wellbeing becomes something that is shared rather than carried alone.

For those of us working in trauma-exposed systems, it can make the difference between simply surviving the work and being able to stay, grow and continue showing up in ways that feel human, sustainable and connected to who we are.

Strengths interventions for the trauma-informed practitioner

The following interventions are drawn from positive psychology research and are particularly helpful for practitioners working in complex, emotionally demanding environments.

Find out your signature strengths

The first intervention I'll mention is to take some time to identify your signature strengths.

Research highlights that simply knowing our strengths can enhance our wellbeing, increase self-acceptance and result in more positive experiences at work (Niemiec, 2018). Strengths awareness can also support problem-solving, particularly in stressful moments, by reminding us that we have internal resources to lean on when things feel difficult.

One way to identify your character strengths is to complete the free VIA Character Strengths Survey, available online. While the survey itself can be helpful, the real value comes from reflection.

You might like to consider:

- Where do these strengths show up in my work?
- Which strengths feel energising rather than depleting?
- Which strengths help regulate me when I'm stressed or under pressure?
- Which strengths do others regularly recognise in me?

Strengths spotting

We discussed strengths spotting earlier in this chapter. It involves noticing and naming the strengths we see in other people. This can be a powerful and connective practice to share within a team. When done intentionally, strengths spotting helps build trust, strengthen relationships and counter the tendency to focus only on what is going wrong (Niemiec, 2018; Peterson & Seligman, 2004). It also provides meaningful positive feedback – something that is often scarce in trauma-affected systems.

A simple way to structure a strengths spotting round includes three steps:

1. Name a strength you have noticed in someone else.
2. Share a specific example of that strength in action.
3. Explain why you appreciate this strength and the positive impact it has had on you, the team or the wider community.

This practice supports the development of a more balanced narrative within teams. People begin to see how their strengths positively influence the culture around them, reinforcing a sense of contribution and belonging, both individually and collectively.

You at your best

The you at your best intervention invites reflection on a time when you were functioning and feeling at your best. This can be done as a personal writing exercise or as a storytelling activity with others.

It's most effective when we are descriptive and unpack the details:

- What exactly were we doing at the time?
- Where were we, and what situation were we in?
- Who were we with?
- What role did we play for them, or did they play for us?
- How did we feel?
- What helped us to be at our best?

When we unpack these details, our strengths become easier to see. We begin to recognise the qualities we were drawing on – perhaps our perseverance, humour, kindness, leadership, creativity, fairness or social intelligence. Reflecting on ourselves at our best reminds us that these strengths are within us, ready to be drawn on when we need them most.

Using strengths in new and novel ways

Once we have spent some time getting to know our signature strengths, we can then explore new and novel ways to use them. This intervention comes directly from positive psychology research and is one of the most effective ways to increase wellbeing and reduce symptoms of burnout or stress (Seligman et al., 2005; Niemiec, 2018).

Here's what to do:

1. Choose one of your signature strengths.
2. For one week, intentionally find a *new* way to use that strength. It doesn't need to be big or time-consuming. For example:
    - If your strength is gratitude, express gratitude to someone you don't usually thank.
    - If your strength is humour, use a light moment to ease tension in a meeting.
    - If your strength is love of learning, listen to a short podcast on your commute.

- If your strength is kindness, leave an encouraging note on a colleague's desk.

This practice reconnects us with the parts of ourselves that feel energising and authentic, especially on days that feel demanding. In trauma-exposed work, where stress responses can so easily become habitual, intentionally using our strengths in fresh ways helps widen both our emotional and cognitive flexibility, offering us new pathways back to steadiness and possibility.

As we begin to reconnect with our strengths, something else often starts to come into focus: not just what we are capable of, but why this work matters to us in the first place. For many of us in trauma-affected roles, our strengths are closely tied to our sense of purpose. They show up in the moments when we care deeply, persist when things are hard, advocate when it would be easier to stay quiet or continue to show up for people who need consistency more than perfection.

Meaning (but make it sustainable)

For many of us working in trauma-affected spaces, meaning is not hard to find. We're likely drawn to the work because it matters, and it can make a difference in the lives of the people we support. We believe deeply in children, young people, families and communities. We often work in radical and relational ways within systems that do not always believe in them in the same way we do.

From a positive psychology perspective, meaning in life refers to the felt sense that our lives and experiences make sense and matter (Steger, 2009). It is about coherence, significance and contribution.

In wellbeing science, meaning and purpose are closely linked to positive functioning. They support our capacity to cope, persist and stay engaged. Research consistently shows that people who find their work meaningful report greater life satisfaction, lower stress, fewer physical complaints and stronger psychological wellbeing. Meaningful work is associated with higher motivation, resilience and a deeper sense of engagement, particularly in challenging professions.

Importantly, purpose does not have to be grand or world-changing. It can live in the everyday choices that allow us to contribute in ways that feel meaningful to us, whether that is caring for family, supporting a team, teaching young people, creating something beautiful or simply making life a little lighter for someone else.

Research led by Dr Tom Brunzell and colleagues explored how teachers experience meaningful work in trauma-impacted classrooms. Their findings confirmed what many educators intuitively know: this work is deeply meaningful, and that meaning is often drawn from relationships, pedagogy and the sense of contributing to something larger than oneself (Brunzell et al., 2018).

But importantly, the study also found that meaningful work and teacher wellbeing are closely linked. When teachers' wellbeing is compromised, their experience of meaning is compromised too. Meaning does not sit neatly on top of stress as a protective layer. It is shaped by the conditions in which the work is done.

In trauma-affected work, meaning is often what draws us in and what keeps us going. But it is also something systems can lean on, sometimes unintentionally, to justify unsustainable workloads and emotional labour.

So meaning has a shadow side.

When I moved into school leadership, I carried a deep sense of responsibility for the staff and students I was leading. The work felt urgent and important, and I believed that being a good leader meant putting others first, always. I prioritised my team, my students, and the needs of the school over my personal life, my rest, and often my own wellbeing. At the time, it felt justified. The work mattered too much to do anything else.

Michael Steger's (2009) research reminds us that meaning supports wellbeing best when it is paired with fit, support and realistic conditions. Meaning alone cannot compensate for chronic overwhelm. Brunzell et al.'s (2018) work reinforces this from a trauma-informed viewpoint. While meaningful work can buffer stress, it is not protective enough to counteract systems that rely on goodwill instead of sustainable structures.

Human nervous systems cannot run on purpose alone. Meaning becomes sustainable when it is paired with supportive cultures, realistic expectations and leadership that models boundaries rather than martyrdom.

So as you reflect on your own sense of purpose, I invite you to hold two questions gently, side-by-side:

- What gives this work meaning for me?
- What needs to be in place so that this meaning does not cost me my wellbeing?

Meaning-based interventions for the trauma-informed practitioner

The following interventions are designed to help practitioners reconnect with purpose in ways that are flexible, sustainable and protective of wellbeing, particularly in trauma-exposed roles.

Symbols of purpose

One of the most helpful practices I return to, both personally and with teams, is revisiting our *why* story.

I often invite people to reflect on an object, image or symbol that represents their *why*. For me, it is the tattoo on my arm: a tree with a tyre swing. It is a dedication to my grandparents, the adults who believed in my future and created a childhood that felt safe, playful and full of possibility. It reminds me why I do this work.

When we share these symbols with colleagues, meaning becomes relational. What was once held internally is now recognised and supported by others. This shared recognition can strengthen our sense of purpose and help it endure over time. In trauma-exposed settings where people often carry a great deal alone, having meaning held collectively can be deeply protective.

Circles of contribution

In trauma-exposed work, it is common for practitioners to absorb responsibility that extends far beyond their role. When systems struggle, individuals often try to compensate. Over time, this can lead to moral injury and exhaustion, and place us at risk of burning out.

The circles of contribution intervention helps clarify where our responsibility begins and ends.

First, draw three concentric circles on a piece of paper. In the inner circle, write: *What is my responsibility?* These are responsibilities that sit clearly within your role, influence, and control.

In the middle circle, write: *What is our responsibility?* These include shared responsibilities that belong to a team, leadership group, or collective.

In the outer circle, write: *What belongs to the system?* These are issues shaped by policy, funding, resourcing or structural decisions beyond your individual control.

Spend time reflecting on where you may be carrying weight that belongs in the outer circles.

The five whys

One particularly helpful way I've found to explore meaning is adapting a practice known as the five whys. Traditionally used in systems thinking to uncover root causes, it can be repurposed here as a reflective tool to gently deepen our understanding of purpose.

Rather than settling for a surface-level answer to *why* we do this work, the invitation is to stay with the question a little longer.

You might begin with a simple response:

Why do I do this work? Because I care about young people, or want to make a difference, or my top value is fairness.

Then, instead of stopping there, you ask again. *Why does that matter to me?*

And then again. And again. And one more time.

Each *why* peels back another layer, often revealing a deeper story.

When purpose is examined rather than assumed, it is less likely to harden into obligation or self-sacrifice. It becomes something we choose, rather than something that quietly demands more than we can give.

As we've explored before, this work is not a marathon. It is a relay. We carry the baton for a time, and then we pass it on. In trauma-informed wellbeing, purpose is not something we use to override our limits.

When meaning is shared, supported, and sustained by healthy systems, it becomes a source of strength.

Chapter summary

- Negativity bias is a normal human feature that once protected our survival as a species, but in modern life it can narrow our thinking, heighten stress and compromise wellbeing.
- In trauma-affected settings, negativity bias can feed a culture of problem-focused thinking, keeping individuals and teams stuck in survival mode.
- Emotions are not 'good' or 'bad'. They are messages, and big emotions in response to big experiences are human and expected.
- Positive emotions help widen our perspective, support connection and increase our capacity to cope and recover.
- Fredrickson's broaden-and-build theory explains that positive emotions broaden our thinking in the moment and, over time, help us build lasting resources.
- Character strengths give us a shared language for 'what's strong within us' and offer evidence-based ways to enhance wellbeing, especially in complex, trauma-exposed work.
- Meaningful work can be a powerful source of resilience in trauma-impacted roles, but meaning is not a protective layer that can compensate for chronic overwhelm or unsafe conditions.

From insight to impact

- **Practise one daily 'What went well, and why?' moment.** At the end of your day, name one thing that went well and why it mattered. Write it down or share it with a colleague. This simple practice helps counter negativity bias and gently trains attention towards what is working.

- **Use one strength on purpose this week.** Identify one of your signature strengths and intentionally use it in a new or slightly different way over the next few days. Notice how it affects your energy, connection or sense of meaning at work.
- **Reframe one recurring problem into a solutions question.** Choose a challenge that keeps coming up and rewrite it as a question that opens possibilities. For example, move from 'Why is this so hard?' to 'What would help this feel more manageable right now?'
- **Create one small ritual that brings positive emotion.** This could be a gratitude note, a moment of humour with a colleague, a short savouring pause or a shared check-in at the end of a meeting. Keep it small, repeatable and realistic within your context.

Conclusion

Imagining What Comes After Survival Mode

All children and young people can have a safe and magical childhood if we have enough safe and supportive adults to support them.

As adults, we're much better placed to offer this support when we are well, and equipped with the knowledge, resources and support to be effective.

Trauma-informed wellbeing cannot be an individual project.

Yes, it asks us to understand ourselves, our nervous systems, our patterns and our needs. But it also asks us to zoom out. To look honestly at the environments we work within and to question the conditions we have come to accept as normal.

As we move beyond survival mode, a bigger question emerges: *What kind of workplaces, teams and systems do we actually want to create?*

For too long, wellbeing has been treated as something to be managed privately – a personal responsibility. A skill to develop in our own time, outside of work hours, often in response to systems that are fundamentally unwell. This framing places the burden on individuals to cope with environments that may be chronically under-resourced, emotionally demanding and misaligned with human needs.

Beyond Survival Mode has invited a different conversation. It asks us to imagine workplaces where wellbeing is not an add-on or simply individual resilience, but the foundation upon which everything else is built. Environments where people are not simply enduring the work, but are supported to grow, connect and contribute over the long-term.

When professionals are thriving, not just surviving, the impact is tangible. There is greater steadiness, more creativity, stronger relationships and a deeper capacity to care. People stay. They collaborate. They recover from challenges rather than accumulating harm.

The complex work becomes more sustainable because it is held differently.

Shifting from surviving to thriving requires us to move away from reactive, burnout-driven responses and towards cultures that are intentionally designed to support people before they reach breaking point. This includes realistic workloads, relational leadership, clear boundaries, shared responsibility and systems that recognise the emotional labour inherent in trauma-affected work.

This is the work of NEST in action. We notice the early signs of strain before crisis hits. We embed rhythms and structures that make wellbeing sustainable rather than aspirational. We strengthen the relational fabric of our teams so that no one is holding complexity alone. And we create the conditions for thriving, where creativity, belonging and meaning are not accidental, but designed for.

This becomes our collective responsibility.

Trauma-informed wellbeing asks leaders to model boundaries rather than martyrdom. It asks teams to care for one another, and it asks systems to take responsibility for the conditions they create, rather than outsourcing wellbeing to individuals under the banner of resilience.

As we look to the future of trauma-informed wellbeing, the question is not only 'What can I do differently?' but 'What can we do together?'

In your role, this might look like advocating for safer workloads, creating space for reflection and connection, challenging narratives that glorify self-sacrifice, or designing policies and practices that centre wellbeing as a core value. Or it may mean naming when something is no longer sustainable, supporting colleagues to step back without shame, or using your voice to influence change at a broader level.

None of this happens overnight. Systems change is slow, relational and often uncomfortable. But it begins with a shared vision.

A vision of workplaces where people are allowed to be human. Where care flows in all directions. Where wellbeing is something we build together so that fewer people have to live in survival mode in the first place.

Trauma-informed wellbeing is, ultimately, a collective act.

And the future of this work depends not on how much individuals can endure, but on how willing we are to change the systems that shape our lives, our work and our capacity to thrive.

References

Akdağ, B., Çelebi, S. B., İpekten, F., Usluoğlu, F., & Nasıroğlu, S. (2023). The moderating role of posttraumatic growth in secondary traumatic stress–burnout relationship: A sample of child psychiatrists from Turkey. *Middle East Current Psychiatry, 30,* 93.

Algoe, S. B. (2012). Find, remind, and bind: The functions of gratitude in everyday relationships. *Social and Personality Psychology Compass, 6*(6), 455–469.

Allen, K. A., Kern, M. L., Vella-Brodrick, D., Hattie, J., & Waters, L. (2018). What schools need to know about fostering school belonging: A meta-analysis. *Educational Psychology Review, 30*(1), 1–34.

Allen, T. D., Eby, L. T., Poteet, M. L., Lentz, E., & Lima, L. (2004). Career benefits associated with mentoring for protégés: A meta-analysis. *Journal of Applied Psychology, 89*(1), 127–136.

American Psychological Association. (n.d.). *Emotion.* APA Dictionary of Psychology. https://dictionary.apa.org/emotion

Aron, A., Melinat, E., Aron, E. N., Vallone, R. D., & Bator, R. J. (1997). The experimental generation of interpersonal closeness: A procedure and some preliminary findings. *Personality and Social Psychology Bulletin, 23*(4), 363–377.

Arthurson, S., Lohmeyer, B., & Riggs, D. W. (2025). Foster carer experiences of vicarious trauma: A qualitative interpretive meta-synthesis. *Children and Youth Services Review, 176,* 108421.

Australian Bureau of Statistics. (2022). *National study of mental health and wellbeing, 2020–2021.* https://www.abs.gov.au/statistics/health/mental-health/national-study-mental-health-and-wellbeing/latest-release

Australian Institute of Health and Welfare. (2022). *Australia's health 2022: Mental health.* https://www.aihw.gov.au/reports/australias-health/mental-health

Bandura, A. (1997). *Self-efficacy: The exercise of control.* W. H. Freeman.

Baumeister, R. F., Bratslavsky, E., Finkenauer, C., & Vohs, K. D. (2001). Bad is stronger than good. *Review of General Psychology, 5*(4), 323–370.

Baumeister, R. F., & Leary, M. R. (1995). The need to belong: Desire for interpersonal attachments as a fundamental human motivation. *Psychological Bulletin, 117*(3), 497–529.

Beacon House Therapeutic Services & Trauma Team. (2020). *Building emotional regulation skills in children & young people: Module two training notes.* Beacon House Therapeutic Services.

Biswas-Diener, R., Kashdan, T. B., & Minhas, G. (2011). A dynamic approach to psychological strength development and intervention. *The Journal of Positive Psychology, 6*(2), 106–118.

Boulton, M. J., & Smith, P. K. (1992). The social nature of play fighting and play chasing: Mechanisms and strategies underlying cooperation and compromise. *Aggressive Behavior, 18*(2), 141–157.

Bowen, E. A., & Murshid, N. S. (2016). Trauma-informed social policy: A conceptual framework for policy analysis and advocacy. *American Journal of Public Health, 106*(2), 223–229.

Bowlby, J. (1980). *Attachment and loss: Vol. 3. Loss.* Basic Books.

Bride, B. E. (2007). Prevalence of secondary traumatic stress among social workers. *Social Work, 52*(1), 63–70.

Bride, B. E., Radey, M., & Figley, C. R. (2007). Measuring compassion fatigue. *Clinical Social Work Journal, 35*(3), 155–163.

Brokenleg, M. (1998). Native wisdom on belonging. *Reclaiming Children and Youth, 7*(3).

Brown, B. (2010). *The gifts of imperfection: Let go of who you think you're supposed to be and embrace who you are.* Hazelden Publishing.

Brown, B. (2018). *Dare to lead: Brave work. Tough conversations. Whole hearts.* Random House.

Brown, S. (2009). *Play: How it shapes the brain, opens the imagination, and invigorates the soul.* Avery.

Brunzell, T., Stokes, H., & Waters, L. (2018). Why do you work with struggling students? Teacher perceptions of meaningful work in trauma-impacted classrooms. *Australian Journal of Teacher Education, 43*(2).

Bryant, F. B. (2021). Savoring. In M. L. Kern & M. L. Wehmeyer (Eds.), *The Palgrave encyclopedia of positive psychology.* Palgrave Macmillan.

Bryant, F. B., & Veroff, J. (2007). *Savoring: A new model of positive experience.* Lawrence Erlbaum Associates.

Bryk, A. S., & Schneider, B. (2002). *Trust in schools: A core resource for improvement.* Russell Sage Foundation.

Cale, J., Dowling, C., & Leclerc, B. (2022). Childhood maltreatment among justice-involved youth in Australia: Prevalence and implications. *Australian & New Zealand Journal of Criminology, 55*(3), 420–438.

Caringi, J. C., Hardiman, E. R., Weldon, P., Fletcher, S., Devlin, M., & Stanick, C. (2016). Secondary traumatic stress and licensed clinical social workers. *Traumatology*. Advance online publication.

Cerritelli, F., Frasch, M. G., Antonelli, M. C., Renzetti, C., Cozzolino, V., & Barlafante, G. (2021). A review on the vagus nerve and autonomic nervous system during fetal development: Searching for critical windows. *Frontiers in Neuroscience, 15*, 721605.

Cockshaw, W. D., & Shochet, I. M. (2010). The link between belongingness and depressive symptoms: An exploration in the workplace interpersonal context. *Australian Psychologist, 45*(4), 283–289.

Costello, B., Wachtel, J., & Wachtel, T. (2010). *Restorative circles in schools: Building community and enhancing learning.* International Institute for Restorative Practices.

Deci, E. L., & Ryan, R. M. (2000). The 'what' and 'why' of goal pursuits: Human needs and the self-determination of behavior. *Psychological Inquiry, 11*(4), 227–268.

Dolhinow, P., & Bishop, N. H. (1970). The development of motor skills and social interactions among primates. *Folia Primatologica, 12*(3–4), 165–178.

Edmondson, A. (1999). Psychological safety and learning behavior in work teams. *Administrative Science Quarterly, 44*(2), 350–383.

Edmondson, A. C., & Harvey, J. F. (2018). Cross-boundary teaming for innovation: Integrating research on teams and knowledge in organizations. *Human Resource Management Review, 28*(4), 347–360.

Eisenberger, N. I., Lieberman, M. D., & Williams, K. D. (2003). Does rejection hurt? An fMRI study of social exclusion. *Science, 302*(5643), 290–292.

Emmons, R. A., & McCullough, M. E. (2003). Counting blessings versus burdens: An experimental investigation of gratitude and subjective well-being in daily life. *Journal of Personality and Social Psychology, 84*(2), 377–389.

Figley, C. R. (2002). Compassion fatigue: Psychotherapists' chronic lack of self-care. *Journal of Clinical Psychology, 58*(11), 1433–1441.

Franco, C., Murrie, D. C., & Vincent, G. M. (2013). Serious juvenile offenders: Prevalence of childhood adversity and its relationship to risk for reoffending. *Psychology, Public Policy, and Law, 19*(2), 207–218.

Fraser, A., & Molineux, J. (2025). *The silent cost: Impact and management of secondary trauma in educators* (Report). The Flourish Movement.

Fredrickson, B. L. (1998). What good are positive emotions? *Review of General Psychology, 2*(3), 300–319.

Fredrickson, B. L. (2001). The role of positive emotions in positive psychology: The broaden-and-build theory of positive emotions. *American Psychologist, 56*(3), 218–226.

Fredrickson, B. L. (2004). The broaden-and-build theory of positive emotions. *Philosophical Transactions of the Royal Society B: Biological Sciences, 359*(1449), 1367–1377.

Fredrickson, B. L. (2013). *Love 2.0: Creating happiness and health in moments of connection.* Hudson Street Press.

Fredrickson, B. L., & Algoe, S. B. (2012). Positive emotions. In C. R. Snyder & S. J. Lopez (Eds.), *The Oxford handbook of positive psychology* (2nd ed.). Oxford University Press.

Gallup Australia. (2023). *State of the global workplace 2023 report.* https://www.gallup.com/workplace/349484/state-of-the-global-workplace.aspx

Garfin, D. R., Silver, R. C., & Holman, E. A. (2020). The novel coronavirus (COVID-19) outbreak: Amplification of public health consequences by media exposure. *Health Psychology, 39*(5), 355–357.

Goleman, D. (2006). *Social intelligence: The new science of human relationships.* Bantam Books.

Govindji, R., & Linley, P. A. (2007). Strengths use, self-concordance and well-being: Implications for strengths coaching and coaching psychologists. *International Coaching Psychology Review, 2*(2), 143–153.

Greene, R. W. (2008). *Lost at school: Why our kids with behavioral challenges are falling through the cracks and how we can help them.* Scribner.

Gregory, S. Y. (2024, June 13). *Address your stress: Small changes can help make you more resilient.* Mayo Clinic Press. https://mcpress.mayoclinic.org/mental-health/address-your-stress-small-changes-can-help-make-you-more-resilient/

Griffin, B. J., Purcell, N., Burkman, K., Litz, B. T., Bryan, C. J., Schmitz, M., & Maguen, S. (2019). Moral injury: An integrative review. *Journal of Traumatic Stress, 32*(3), 350–362.

Harris, M., & Fallot, R. D. (Eds.). (2001). *Using trauma theory to design service systems.* Jossey-Bass.

Herman, J. (2015). *Trauma and recovery.* Basic Books.

Kahn, R. L., Wolfe, D. M., Quinn, R. P., Snoek, J. D., & Rosenthal, R. A. (1964). *Organizational stress: Studies in role conflict and ambiguity.* Wiley.

Keyes, C. L. M. (2002). The mental health continuum: From languishing to flourishing in life. *Journal of Health and Social Behavior, 43*(2), 207–222.

Keyes, C. L. M. (2024). *Languishing: How to feel alive again in a world that wears us down.* Penguin Random House Australia.

Keyes, C. L. M., & Annas, J. (2009). Feeling good and functioning well: Distinctive concepts in ancient philosophy and contemporary science. *The Journal of Positive Psychology, 4*(3), 197–201.

Koloroutis, M., & Pole, N. (2021). Trauma-informed leadership. *Nursing Management, 52*(12).

Kram, K. E. (1985). *Mentoring at work: Developmental relationships in organizational life.* Scott, Foresman and Company.

Langley-Freeman, M., Langton, G., & Brunzell, T. (2023). Deepening understandings of our stress-responses: Empowering students to become ready to learn. *Education Today.* https://www.educationtoday.com.au/news-detail/Deepening-Understand-6002

Lelorain, S., Bonnaud-Antignac, A., & Florin, A. (2010). Long term posttraumatic growth after breast cancer: Prevalence, predictors and relationships with psychological health. *Journal of Clinical Psychology in Medical Settings, 17*(1), 14–22.

Levine, P. A. (2010). *In an unspoken voice: How the body releases trauma and restores goodness.* North Atlantic Books.

Linley, P. A., Nielsen, K. M., Wood, A. M., Gillett, R., & Biswas-Diener, R. (2010). Using signature strengths in pursuit of goals. *Journal of Happiness Studies, 11,* 83–103.

Litz, B. T., Stein, N., Delaney, E., Lebowitz, L., Nash, W. P., Silva, C., & Maguen, S. (2009). Moral injury and moral repair in war veterans: A preliminary model and intervention strategy. *Clinical Psychology Review, 29*(8), 695–706.

Lloyd, R. C. (2024). Trauma-informed leadership: Integrating research-based leadership theories and SAMHSA principles for building resilient teams. In *Regent Research Roundtables Proceedings* (pp. 288–303). Regent University School of Business & Leadership.

Louis, K. S., Dretzke, B., & Wahlstrom, K. (2010). How does leadership affect student achievement? Results from a national US survey. *School Effectiveness and School Improvement, 21*(3), 315–336.

Lutz, A., Brefczynski-Lewis, J., Johnstone, T., & Davidson, R. J. (2008). Regulation of the neural circuitry of emotion by compassion meditation: Effects of meditative expertise. *PLoS ONE, 3*(3), e1897.

Malvaso, C. G., Day, A., Cale, A., Hackett, J., Delfabbro, L., Ross, P., & Stuart, S. (2022). *Adverse childhood experiences and trauma among young people in the youth justice system* (Trends & Issues in Crime and Criminal Justice No. 651). Australian Institute of Criminology.

Manning-Jones, S., de Terte, I., & Stephens, C. (2015). Vicarious posttraumatic growth: A systematic literature review. *International Journal of Wellbeing, 5*(2), 125–139.

Martin, R. A. (2007). *The psychology of humor: An integrative approach.* Elsevier.

Maslach, C., & Leiter, M. P. (2016). Understanding the burnout experience: Recent research and its implications for psychiatry. *World Psychiatry, 15*(2), 103–111

Maté, G. (2021). Recovering from helper syndrome: Five levels of compassion to foster growth as therapists. *Psychotherapy Networker.* https://www.psychotherapynetworker.org/article/helper-syndrome/

Molnar, B. E., Meeker, S. A., Manners, K., Tieszen, L., Kalergis, K., Fine, J. E., Hallinan, S., Wolfe, J. D., & Wells, M. K. (2020). Vicarious traumatization among child welfare and child protection professionals: A systematic review. *Child Abuse & Neglect, 110*(Pt 3), 104679.

Mols, F., Vingerhoets, A. J., Coebergh, J. W., & van de Poll-Franse, L. V. (2009). Well-being, posttraumatic growth and benefit finding in long-term breast cancer survivors. *Psycho-Oncology, 18*(6), 577–585.

Morrison, B., & Vaandering, D. (2012). *Restorative justice: Pedagogy, praxis, and discipline.* Palgrave Macmillan.

Murray, D. W., Rosanbalm, K., Christopoulos, C., & Hamoudi, A. (2015). *Self-regulation and toxic stress: Foundations for understanding self-regulation from an applied developmental perspective.* Office of Planning, Research and Evaluation, Administration for Children and Families, US Department of Health and Human Services.

Neff, K. D. (2003). Self-compassion: An alternative conceptualization of a healthy attitude toward oneself. *Self and Identity, 2*, 85-102.

Neff, K. D., & Germer, C. (2017). Self-compassion and psychological wellbeing. In J. Doty (Ed.), *Oxford handbook of compassion science*, Oxford University Press.

Niemiec, R. M. (2018). *Character strengths interventions: A field guide for practitioners.* Hogrefe.

Niemiec, R. M., & McGrath, R. E. (2019). *The power of character strengths: Appreciate and ignite your positive personality.* VIA Institute on Character.

Perry, B. D. (2006) The Neurosequential Model of Therapeutics: Applying principles of neuroscience to clinical work with traumatized and maltreated children. In Nancy Boyd Webb (Ed.), *Working with traumatized youth in child welfare* (pp. 27–52), The Guilford Press.

Perry, B. D., & Szalavitz, M. (2017). *The boy who was raised as a dog* (Rev. ed.). Basic Books.

Peterson, C. (2008). *What is positive psychology?* Oxford University Press.

Peterson, C., & Seligman, M. E. P. (2004). *Character strengths and virtues: A handbook and classification.* Oxford University Press.

Polyvagal Institute. (n.d.). *What is polyvagal theory?* https://www.polyvagalinstitute.org/whatispolyvagaltheory

Porges, S. W. (2007). The polyvagal perspective. *Biological Psychology, 74*(2).

Reavis, J. A., Looman, J., Franco, K. A., & Rojas, B. (2013). Adverse childhood experiences and adult criminality: How long must we live before we possess our own lives? *The Permanente Journal, 17*(2), 44–48.

Reinhardt, C. (2016). *Compassion fatigue and compassion satisfaction in foster carers: A mixed methods approach* (Master's thesis). University of Limerick.

Remen, R. N. (1996). *Kitchen table wisdom: Stories that heal.* Riverhead Books.

Robson, R. (2025). *Why trauma-informed leadership is the next evolution in psychological safety.* Australian HR Institute. https://www.ahri.com.au/articles/trauma-informed-leadership-next-evolution-psychological-safety

Rogers, C. R. (1951). *Client-centered therapy: Its current practice, implications, and theory.* Houghton Mifflin.

Rozin, P., & Royzman, E. B. (2001). Negativity bias, negativity dominance, and contagion. *Personality and Social Psychology Review, 5*(4), 296–320.

Saakvitne, K. W., & Pearlman, L. A. (1996). *Transforming the pain: A workbook on vicarious traumatization.* W. W. Norton & Company.

SAMHSA (Substance Abuse and Mental Health Services Administration). (2014). *SAMHSA's concept of trauma and guidance for a trauma-informed approach* (HHS Publication No. SMA 14-4884). U.S. Department of Health and Human Services.

Sarmiento, L. F., Lopes da Cunha, P., Tabares, S., Tafet, G., & Gouveia, A., Jr. (2024). Decision-making under stress: A psychological and neurobiological integrative model. *Brain, Behavior, & Immunity – Health, 38*, 100766.

Seligman, M. E. P., Steen, T. A., Park, N., & Peterson, C. (2005). Positive psychology progress: Empirical validation of interventions. *American Psychologist, 60*(5), 410–421.

Siegel, D. J. (2012). *The developing mind: How relationships and the brain interact to shape who we are* (2nd ed.). Guilford Press.

Steger, M. F. (2009). Meaning in life. In S. J. Lopez (Ed.), *The encyclopedia of positive psychology* (pp. 605–610). Wiley-Blackwell.

Tervalon, M., & Murray-García, J. (1998). Cultural humility versus cultural competence: A critical distinction in defining physician training outcomes in multicultural education. *Journal of Health Care for the Poor and Underserved, 9*(2), 117–125.

Vaish, A., Grossmann, T., & Woodward, A. (2008). Not all emotions are created equal: The negativity bias in social-emotional development. *Psychological Bulletin, 134*(3), 383–403.

van der Kolk, B. (2014). *The body keeps the score.* Viking.

Waldinger, R. J. (2023). *The good life: Lessons from the world's longest scientific study of happiness.* Simon & Schuster.

Waldinger, R. J., & Schulz, M. S. (2010). What makes a good life? Lessons from the longest study on happiness. *Psychiatric Times, 27*(12), 1–3.

Wasilewski, M. B., Rios, J., Simpson, R., Hitzig, S. L., Gotlib Conn, L., MacKay, C., Mayo, A. L., & Robinson, L. R. (2023). Peer support for traumatic injury survivors: A scoping review. *Disability and Rehabilitation, 45*(13), 2199–2232.

Wild, N. D., & Paivio, S. C. (2003). Psychological adjustment, coping, and emotion regulation as predictors of posttraumatic growth. *Journal of Aggression, Maltreatment & Trauma, 8*(4), 97–122.

Williamson, V., Stevelink, S. A. M., & Greenberg, N. (2018). Occupational moral injury and mental health: Systematic review and meta-analysis. *The British Journal of Psychiatry, 212*(6), 339–346.

Wood, A. M., Froh, J. J., & Geraghty, A. W. A. (2010). Gratitude and well-being: A review and theoretical integration. *Clinical Psychology Review, 30*(7), 890–905.

Acknowledgements

This book was written while travelling across various lands, including the lands of the Bunurong People, Gadubanud People and Wurundjeri People of the South East Kulin Nation. I wish to acknowledge the Traditional Custodians of these lands and pay my respects to their Elders past and present. Living, playing, working and writing on these lands is a privilege.

I owe the biggest thank you to my beautiful grandparents, Max and Phyl, who provided me with a safe and magical childhood and believed in my future.

I'd like to thank all the children and young people I have had the pleasure to walk alongside as an educator. Thank you for frequently making me laugh, pushing me to be a better educator and human being, and teaching me more than you realise. You are the reason this book exists.

I'd like to thank Kosta, who patiently cheered me on as this book came to life. For believing in me all the way through, and for being the first to read a chapter or two. This book would not exist without you.

Thank you to little Yuki, who was by my side through the whole process.

A special thank you to those who reviewed the book. It's such an important, and vulnerable, part of the process. To Tom, Jack, Annemarie, Ben, Thea, Richard and Marg. I am so grateful. You were the absolute best people to take this on!

Thank you to the wonderful people I have worked alongside over my career. There are so many brilliant professionals I met during my years at Berry Street, Collingwood Alternative School, and Saint Joe's. We certainly brought the 'peer support' benefits to life. Special mention to my mentors, Graeme, Chris and Sue. (Sue, thanks for taking a chance on me as a young graduate teacher!)

I continue to meet so many amazing professionals through my work with Wagtail Institute, too. Thank you to everyone who puts up their hand to support children and young people on their journey, and who are always seeking best practices and sustainable ways to do it. You all continue to inspire me.

I must mention my informal writing group, too: ... and wellbeing. Thanks Paul, Kesh and Jack for creating a safe space to truly be myself and to play with my writing along the way. ... and wellbeing is special!

Thank you to my beautiful friends and family who encouraged me, offered support and cheered me on along the way, too, from my MAPPsters, to my boxing community, my colleagues, the volunteers and family in Nablus, and those who've been there since we were children and young people, too. Thank you for being a special part of my journey.

And of course, the biggest thank you to Alicia, Brooke and the Amba Press team for believing in this book, for offering incredible support along the way, and for bringing this book to life!

www.ingramcontent.com/pod-product-compliance
Lightning Source LLC
LaVergne TN
LVHW052326200926
848481LV00002B/681
* 9 7 8 1 9 2 3 4 0 3 7 2 7 *